PRACTICAL UX

PRACTICAL UX

A Hands-on Guide to Getting Industry-Recognized Experience

Maigen Thomas

MERCURY LEARNING AND INFORMATION
Boston, Massachusetts

MERCURY LEARNING AND INFORMATION
121 High Street, 3rd Floor
Boston, MA 02110
info@merclearning.com

M. Thomas. *Practical UX: A Hands-on Guide to Getting Industry-Recognized Experience.*
ISBN: 978-1-50152-347-2

Library of Congress Control Number: 2025930991

242526321   This book is printed on acid-free paper in the United States of America.

For Jason Nash, Tanisa Imoto, Amy Eden Jollymore, Meg Foley, Seth Yount and the Creeps. If y'all didn't already know how awesome I think you are, now you do. Thank you for your unwavering belief in me.

CONTENTS

INTRODUCTION

The job market for early-career UX (user experience) designers presents unique challenges in today's digital landscape. The industry layoffs of 2022–2024, combined with the increasing number of bootcamp graduates entering the workforce, have created unprecedented competition for entry-level positions. While companies continue to list roles requiring 3–5 years of experience, most candidates seeking work are what industry professionals consider "true juniors"—those with less than one year of working experience.

This guide offers a practical solution to a common problem: how to gain real-world, industry-recognized experience when companies are not hiring junior designers. Through a structured, actionable approach, this book will teach you how to:

- Identify and approach potential clients who need your services
- Conduct professional website evaluations focusing on accessibility and usability
- Create meaningful presentations that demonstrate your value
- Build compelling case studies that showcase real impact
- Price and deliver your services effectively

WHY FOCUS ON ACCESSIBILITY?

Accessibility-focused design is not merely a trend—it represents both a critical business necessity and a significant market opportunity. Consider these compelling statistics:

- Approximately 11,000 Americans turn 65 each day
- 26% of the United States population lives with some form of disability
- Globally, nearly 1.4 billion people have disabilities—a market the size of China
- The spending power of people with disabilities and their networks exceeds $13 trillion annually

Moreover, recent legal requirements in the United States and the European Union mandate that publicly available websites must be accessible to all users, including those with disabilities. This regulatory shift has created an urgent need for designers who understand accessibility principles and can implement them effectively.

THE PRACTICAL UX APPROACH

This book presents a systematic method for gaining professional experience while delivering real value to businesses. Each chapter builds upon the previous one, leading you through a complete project cycle:

1. Finding the right size business to work with
2. Approaching potential clients professionally
3. Selling your services confidently
4. Conducting thorough website evaluations
5. Creating impactful presentations
6. Delivering professional results
7. Building compelling case studies

The methodology focuses specifically on small businesses and their websites, where you can make meaningful improvements that directly impact business metrics. This approach allows you to:

- Work with real businesses solving real problems
- Build a portfolio of actual client work

- Develop crucial client communication skills
- Generate income while gaining experience
- Create case studies that demonstrate business impact

WHO THIS BOOK IS FOR

This guide serves several groups of early-career digital professionals:

- Recent UX/UI bootcamp graduates seeking their first roles
- Career-changers building their portfolios
- Self-taught designers requiring real-world experience
- Junior designers looking to specialize in accessibility
- Freelancers wanting to expand their service offerings

HOW TO USE THIS BOOK

Each chapter provides specific, actionable steps along with supplementary materials, templates, and scripts. The book is designed to be worked through sequentially, though experienced practitioners may choose to focus on specific chapters relevant to their immediate needs.

The supplementary materials include:

- Client outreach tracking templates
- A website evaluation spreadsheet
- A presentation slide deck template
- Professional documentation templates
- Communication scripts and email templates

By following this guide, you will not only gain valuable professional experience but also be able to help businesses become more accessible and inclusive while protecting them from potential legal issues. The skills you develop through this process will prove invaluable throughout your career in user experience design.

This book will serve as a roadmap for gaining real-world experience in UX design, with a focus on accessibility—one of the most pressing needs in digital design today. Let us begin with finding the right size business for your first project.

AUTHOR NOTE

You have made an excellent choice in purchasing this book. It may seem small, but this book is packed full of valuable, career-transforming, confidence-building, actionable advice. This book is going to teach you a very specific set of skills, in a very particular order. If you follow this process, you will not only learn how to get real-world, industry recognized experience, you will learn new skills and develop an aptitude for exercising a truly future-focused, highly compensated skill.

In Chapter 1, you will select a target customer. A client that is not too big and not too small. A client that is just right for your current level of skill and knowledge. Identifying the right size of challenge is a skill that will serve you well in the future. Being able to recognize when you have the energy and time to "surge" to meet high expectations and lofty goals, as well as being able to recognize when you need to aim a little more realistically—this is a level of self-awareness few people develop. You'll figure out why focusing on things you're interested in is important for maintaining long-term motivation, and why starting with a smaller, more local company makes it easier to get paid to get experience. By the end of this chapter, you will have created an outreach list of potential clients, have a strategy for building relationships with them, and clear boundaries for the projects you choose to take on.

In Chapter 2, you will focus on developing your marketing pitch. You'll learn how to recognize a healthy company that is on target to meet their goals, a company where you can enhance their success rather than trying to rescue an organization that is beyond help. You will get familiar with your strengths and learn how to communicate the value you can bring that can impact a company's bottom line. You'll learn how to talk about what you do confidently and create your personal script to make it easy. By the end of this chapter, you will be able to understand your target customer's business goals and success metrics "at a glance" and be able to describe why your work can reduce costs or increase revenue.

Chapter 3 is where you will learn how to sell your services to a potential customer. We will go into detail about what service you can provide that a small business will not only value but pay for. You will learn how to ask for their business and how to handle their response, whether it is a "yes" or a "no." Once you have finished this chapter you will be prepared to confidently approach an ideal potential customer, know exactly what to say, and handle the outcome gracefully.

In Chapter 4, we get down to the proverbial brass tacks. This chapter focuses on the repeatable process of evaluating the usability and accessibility of a website, looking for friction points that turn off potential customers and expose the business to digital accessibility lawsuits. This chapter also covers essential practices like conducting a detailed stakeholder interview, identifying primary user goals, and using a comprehensive evaluation tool to identify accessibility barriers that impact the experiences of people with disabilities. By the end of this chapter, you will have a new process for interviewing stakeholders, a method for identifying the business goals of any organization, a repeatable strategy for evaluating a website and a robust rubric for understanding and documenting the severity of accessibility barriers on a website.

Chapter 5 is where we synthesize our findings and make informed recommendations for real, practical improvements to a website. We will discuss how to draw out the most important issues to prioritize based on their level of impact to the most users, and discuss how to suggest the easiest, cheapest way to fix them. Practical knowledge about ranking issues based on impact and communicating how to prioritize the fixes is rare in designers. Being able to bring realistic, money-saving solutions to the table and communicate with simple visual mockups will endear you to future employers. By the end of this chapter, you will know how to document and prioritize accessibility barriers that are identified, prioritize them, and communicate design changes to developers and stakeholders.

In Chapter 6, you will be challenged to expand the boundaries of your comfort zone, stretching into new professional development skills. Chapter 6 focuses on interacting at high levels with stakeholders. Skills include building slide decks, setting up meetings with key decision-makers, presenting confidently, and researching facts that relate to the legal aspects of website accessibility. By the end of this chapter, you will be able to create and deliver a captivating presentation, as well as set up and run an efficient business meeting. You'll also be able to describe business impact in a way that convinces the stakeholder, and proactively suggest next steps that guide the conversation toward buying in on paying you to do the work.

Chapter 7 covers the basics of freelancing and understanding the boundaries of what services you can provide a customer, as well as the legal requirements you need to know about to operate as a freelancer successfully. By the time you complete this chapter you will be able to confidently pitch your services beyond a website evaluation and accurately assess the work you can handle and the work you need to outsource. You will also have a solid plan for finding the legal requirements you need to know about getting paid to provide digital services—including how much to charge for your time and effort.

Finally, in Chapter 8, you will leverage the stakeholder slide deck you created in Chapter 5 to create an accessibility-focused case study for your portfolio. You will be able to identify meaningful impact metrics that make a difference to the business and the real-world impact for the users. You will be able to show the outcomes of your work and not just the output. You will be able to describe the value you can bring to any organization, and why you are a great hire.

Your mission, should you choose to accept it, is to learn a fast, easy, and reliable process for finding the most crucial accessibility issues on any website and create a career-advancing case study so that you can future-proof your career in tech and become the expert who transforms accessibility barriers into inclusive solutions. Your impact will be a more inclusive, human-centered internet experience. Doesn't that sound like a great legacy? It is possible.

If you accept this challenge, turn the page.

CHAPTER 1

FIND THE RIGHT SIZE BUSINESS

Large companies are not hiring junior-level employees for many reasons. Most of the cited reasons can be reduced to an unwillingness to invest in the unknown. While mid- and senior-level employees demand higher salaries, their demonstrated ability to get to know a product and business rapidly is perceived as their key value. Companies want to see a return on their investment in an employee quickly, and mid- and senior-level employees typically prove their worth in a shorter time than junior-level employees do.

As an early-career designer looking to land a salaried role or build a freelance business, it's crucial to demonstrate your ability to perform effectively. To show your abilities to potential hiring managers, you'll need to get industry-recognized experience—the goal of this whole book. Chapter 1 will guide you through a few simple ways to identify potential customers and find a project you're motivated about and excited to work on. By the end of the chapter, you'll have identified at least a dozen potential customers and will be prepared to start reaching out to them, which we'll do in Chapter 2. For now, let's identify the ideal size customer for your skills and offer them a website accessibility evaluation.

WHAT THIS PROCESS TEACHES

This book will help you get experience that you can leverage to get the job that you want. The end-to-end process that *Practical UX* will cover includes:

- How to find a business you can deliver value to at your current skill level
- How to approach the business and pitch your services
- How to sell your service: a low-cost, high-value website evaluation
- How to evaluate a website to identify accessibility barriers and usability issues
- How to make suggestions for improvement that will impact business metrics
- How to prepare a slide deck and report covering your recommendations
- How to deliver a stress-free stakeholder presentation
- How to create a compelling case study for your portfolio

While you are growing your skills as an early-career designer or a career-changer, it's ideal to focus on skills that can transfer to any industry and any type of business. This way, when you land the salaried role you're looking for, you'll have the ability to pivot quickly to pick up the skills you'll need to be successful in that role. Trying to learn all of the skills at the same time makes it impossible to get really good at any one of them. By learning how to evaluate a website for accessibility and usability—and solve accessibility and usability problems through design—you'll be gaining essential skills that ensure you stand out in any pool of candidates.

Why Accessibility-Focused Evaluation and Design Is Important

Accessibility-focused design is not a trend; it's a necessity. The cohort of Americans we call the "Baby Boomer Generation" is rapidly aging. On average, 11,000 people each day in the United States turn 65 years old. Current numbers indicate that about 26% of the United States population has some kind of disability. Globally, the number of people with disabilities is close to 1.4 billion people. That's a market the size of China, and they are all consumers with spending power. These numbers will only increase as the temporarily abled become disabled—and make no mistake; every one of us is only temporarily abled. The United States Census Bureau claims 1 in 5 Americans live with a disability, of which:

- 8.1 million have difficulty seeing
- 2.0 million are completely blind
- 7.6 million have difficulty hearing

- 19.9 million find it difficult to grasp objects (such as a mouse or keyboard)
- 2.4 million live with Alzheimer's disease, senility, or dementia
- 2.8 million live with epilepsy

Solving problems for permanently and chronically disabled users helps all users. It also solves issues for users with temporary disabilities and impairments. Reducing website accessibility barriers helps users with limb differences or a broken hand. It also helps a parent who can't put down a fussy baby. Disabled users are not "edge cases" or one-off problems that do not need to be solved, something that is often argued by development and product teams. Target user groups cannot be segmented or sorted in such a way as to prevent users with disabilities from accessing websites on the internet. It is our responsibility as designers to deliver, by default, accessible websites to enable the companies we work for to reach the most possible customers profitably. Creating accessible interfaces makes that possible.

The evaluation process taught in this book will empower you to identify accessibility barriers and usability issues on websites that typically lead to accessibility lawsuits. (1) An accessibility lawsuit, at minimum, typically costs a small business about $25,000. (2) With what you learn in this book, you can help a small business protect its income and increase its market share. In other words, you can help them make more money and keep more of the money they make. That is a business impact that a hiring manager will be excited to see on your portfolio and resume.

AIM SMALL, MISS SMALL

As an early-career designer looking to get real-world, industry-recognized experience, you'll need to work with a real business to solve real user problems. Many designers think that they need to demonstrate expertise by solving huge problems that impact thousands of people. Not only is this not true, but it is also not beneficial when job searching for junior roles. It is far more valuable to be able to explain why a problem you solved was meaningful for a small business and demonstrate how your work made an impact. The business knowledge gained is applicable throughout your career, regardless of the size of the business or the number of users. This is why *Practical UX* will only focus on helping you work with small businesses. These projects provide powerful experience that often can't be gained when working in larger organizations, with more siloed teams, especially at the beginning of your career.

Made widely known through the 2000 film The Patriot, the phrase "aim small, miss small" is a marksmanship principle that emphasizes focusing on a very specific target to improve accuracy. The idea is that by aiming at a smaller, more precise point, any deviation or miss will be smaller and closer to the intended target. The concept can be applied to our efforts in getting real-world design experience because it encourages setting clear, specific objectives to enhance precision and effectiveness in achieving desired outcomes. Our desired outcome is experience. Larger projects take more time, effort, and resources. Small projects allow us to learn iteratively and rapidly. Therefore, our objective is to get experience through small projects to gain more overall experience that allows us to stand out from other candidates in a crowded market.

How to Right-Size Your First Projects

In every project, there is an opportunity to do a great job and for everything to go perfectly. There is an equal opportunity for things to go poorly and unfold in less desirable ways. The ideal situation for your first client is this: aim to work with a website that is very small.

A simple one-page landing page website is a great choice for your first project. You will be able to follow the entire process of evaluating a website and deliver value even if the website only has one page. Typically, for our first few projects, it is ideal if the website evaluated only has about 5 to 7 pages in total. This means that the evaluation process goes faster, and the synthesis of the evaluation results goes faster. Finding the major opportunities for improvement is also easier and faster. This rapid feedback cycle is perfect for early-career growth.

This recommendation can feel vague, but once you start creating a list of potential clients, which we will do in this chapter, you will have a better idea of what this looks like. You will also feel more comfortable prioritizing potential client projects. Remember, we want to achieve quick wins that help build momentum in our careers. This is not intended to replace your career, merely to get the momentum rolling.

Get Comfortable Delivering Value

When we set the intention to succeed on a small project, we find that we are able to deliver that project quickly and get a sense of whether we are ready to take on a bigger project. What many people do is rush into a much larger project than they can comfortably handle, and then they become overwhelmed. This ultimately undermines their confidence and performance.

For your first 3 to 5 clients, the highest priorities are:

1. Getting comfortable with delivering value
2. Becoming familiar with the accessibility and usability evaluation process

Growing your skills with website evaluation, specifically with regard to accessibility and usability, will benefit your career over the long term more than any other practice. These skills form the foundational knowledge required to be successful as a designer in the future of the technology industry, including adjacent industries that rely on tech products to deliver value to their customers.

This shift in priorities is not just theoretical—it is being driven by legislation. The United States and the European Union have passed laws in the last few years that require publicly available websites to be accessible for all users, including those with disabilities, in the next few years. (3, 4) Previously, the United States only required federal websites to meet a certain level of accessibility. The standards have changed, however, and accessibility will be a key skill that hiring managers look for in candidates going forward. (5)

Focusing on delivering value to small business owners as you carry out accessibility evaluations will build your confidence as you build your skills. By building your expertise around accessibility and usability, you open up opportunities for your career that will not be available to others who focus primarily on visual design. In fact, there are not enough accessibility-focused designers and developers available today across all industries to meet the upcoming demand for accessibility evaluation, design, and development. This is a niche you can build a career focusing on and always be employable.

IDENTIFYING POTENTIAL CUSTOMERS

Before we start looking for potential customers, let's set ourselves up for long-term success by creating a way to track them. You'll find the Potential Client Outreach Tracker Template in the supplemental materials of this book. This is a simple spreadsheet that will become invaluable as we seek out and land our first clients. It will help us better identify businesses we can successfully work with and ensure that our time is spent efficiently.

In your travels across the Internet, you have probably found quite a few websites that are visually displeasing or that provide a sub-optimal user experience. In the past, you might have quickly clicked the back button in your browser and forgotten about it. Going forward, however, you will add these types of websites to your Potential Client Outreach Tracker.

Tracking Your Outreach

You should make this Potential Client Outreach Tracker your own. There are several basic pieces of information tracked, but feel free to add and remove columns if you find you need more or fewer details. For each potential client website you find, you'll want to track a few details. At a minimum, make a note of the name of the company and add the website URL. You might consider adding notes about why it caught your eye and seemed like a potential client, a brief description of the company, and the date you discovered the website. Some additional column data in the spreadsheet will be necessary in the future, such as the date you first reached out or the person you spoke to.

Make a copy of the spreadsheet and start filling these details in as you identify opportunities. Very soon you'll have a list of potential clients you can reach out to in the future. We will be using this spreadsheet for the next two topics in this chapter.

Creating a "Someday Maybe" List

Every time you talk to a small business owner or find a website that needs accessibility support, add it to your tracker. As you continue getting experience and growing in your career, this client outreach tracking template will be available to you whenever you want to take on additional projects, grow your skills, or volunteer your abilities.

Some of the websites you find are not going to be an ideal fit for your immediate needs. Websites with too many pages or that have a lot of dense information may not be customers you can work with right away. Businesses in sectors that are completely unfamiliar to you might seem intimidating to work with. Some websites may be so complex or inaccessible that the project feels too big to take on. Add them to the tracker anyway. David Allen's book, Getthing Things Done: The Art of Stress-Free Productivity introduces the concept of Someday/Maybe

List. This is where you can store the information for businesses you may want to work with in the future, once you've gotten more experience. If it feels appropriate, create a second tab of the spreadsheet and leble it your "Someday Maybe". Now let's gather some potential clients to add to our outreach tracker.

FOLLOW YOUR INTERESTS

As you begin this process to get real-world experience, I recommend that you start creating a list of potential clients by first following your interests. This is a great idea for early-career designers because it is already difficult to move into this industry and career. Why make it more difficult? Our work becomes more difficult when we're not excited about the subject matter. At this point in your career, it is okay to focus on topics that interest you or ignite your curiosity. In fact, doing so will make your outreach to potential customers even easier.

Why They Say "The Riches Are in the Niches"

In the entrepreneurial world, there's a quote: "the riches are in the niches." What this means to entrepreneurs is that rather than trying to be all things to all people, you are likely to find more success by focusing on specific problems to solve for a specific audience.

All you need to do to find businesses in a space you are interested in is to use your favorite search engine. Combine the topic and the words small business, or even just business, and search. In fact, put down this book, open up a search engine, and type in your favorite hobby, type of food, type of clothing, or sport, plus the words small business, and start looking at the resulting websites. Do you notice any design issues on these websites? Put them on your potential client tracker.

Recently, I wanted to take up a new hobby; I wanted to take horseback riding lessons. So, I looked online for horseback riding lessons in my area. I found six options within a reasonable distance and I went to each of their websites. I was looking for Western-style riding, and most of the options near me were English riding only. It might surprise you to know that every single one of the websites was poorly designed. Some of them used display fonts as body text, making it very difficult to read the website. Some of the websites were clearly created many years ago and had not been updated.

It is important to remember that the cost of creating and publishing a website can be as low as $10, or the cost of purchasing a domain.

Many of these small business owners will have created their website themselves using an off-the-shelf tool such as Wix or Squarespace, or they got their niece in high school to create a WordPress website. These small business owners "don't know what they don't know" about website accessibility or the laws requiring their website to be accessible. Even small business websites that have been created on a platform such as Squarespace are not automatically accessible. You might think that because Squarespace is such a big company, they have defaulted to accessible design to protect their customers, but that's not true. I have evaluated many of these platform-based websites and every single one of them had a number of accessibility issues. There are endless opportunities to find a company you can help.

Suggestions For Small Businesses You Can Approach

You're looking for industries where small business owners would benefit from a website accessibility and usability evaluation, but they likely haven't thought about it or invested in it yet. These businesses often serve local or niche markets, rely on their websites to attract customers, and rarely have in-house UX expertise.

Here are just a few examples of potential customers you might consider:

Do you love animals?

Pet-related businesses are everywhere, and many of them have outdated or inaccessible websites. Consider:

- Dog trainers and obedience schools – Small businesses that rely on clear service descriptions and booking systems.
- Pet groomers – Independent groomers often have basic websites with poor accessibility.
- Pet boarding and daycare facilities – Online booking and easy navigation are key for pet owners.
- Mobile veterinarians – Many vets offer at-home services but lack functional sites.
- Custom pet products (collars, accessories, homemade treats, pet clothing) – Many sell through Etsy but could benefit from a full website.

Are you into food?

Food-based businesses are some of the best opportunities for accessibility-focused UX improvements.

- Meal prep services – These businesses rely on clear ordering systems and subscription models.
- Local coffee roasters & specialty tea shops – Often run by small teams who don't have UX knowledge.
- Independent farms & CSAs (Community Supported Agriculture) – Many sell online and could use better navigation.
- Food trucks – Often rely on social media but could benefit from a website for locations and ordering.
- Personal chefs & catering services – Accessibility matters for event planning and dietary needs.

Are you a music fan?

There are plenty of small businesses in the music industry that could use better UX and accessibility:

- Bars, restaurants, and clubs with live music – Many rely on outdated websites for event listings.
- Small music venues – Often have hard-to-navigate event pages and ticketing systems.
- Musical instrument rental shops – These businesses thrive on clear booking and payment processes.
- Amplification & performance equipment rental – Musicians and event organizers need accessible online ordering.
- Lighting, sound, and videography service providers – Many of these businesses serve events and weddings but don't prioritize accessible websites.

Are you passionate about sustainability and eco-friendly living?

Green and eco-conscious businesses are growing, but many have accessibility gaps.

- Zero-waste stores – These shops often have hard-to-navigate sites due to product complexity.

- Solar panel installation companies – Big-ticket items need a strong UX for trust-building.
- Sustainable fashion brands & thrift stores – Many run Shopify stores that lack accessibility.
- Local composting services – Many communities have small businesses offering this but have hard-to-use sites.
- Bike shops & repair businesses – Often run by enthusiasts, not designers, leading to usability issues.

Are you into beauty and fashion?

Small beauty and fashion businesses often rely on visually appealing websites that can lack accessibility:

- Nail technicians and hair stylists – Many have DIY websites that are difficult to navigate.
- Barbershops – Booking and service menus are often visually cluttered.
- Tailors and seamstresses – Many don't have websites at all or only use social media.
- Style advisors and personal shoppers – Their services could benefit from clear, accessible scheduling.
- Virtual assistance & styling services – Online booking and consultations need accessibility improvements.

Do you like education and lifelong learning?

There are many small education-focused businesses that need accessibility help.

- Independent tutors & language teachers – Many have DIY websites that are hard to navigate.
- Small online course creators – Accessibility is crucial for e-learning platforms.
- Music teachers & private instructors – Many rely on simple websites that aren't built with accessibility in mind.
- Children's activity centers (STEM, arts, theater programs) – Parents need easy, accessible booking options.
- Dance studios & martial arts dojos – Registration systems and class schedules often have usability issues.

Do you enjoy gaming or geek culture?

Gaming-related small businesses often have clunky, inaccessible websites.

- Tabletop gaming shops & board game cafés – Many have outdated websites for event booking.
- Escape room businesses – These rely on online reservations but often struggle with accessibility.
- Custom PC builders & repair shops – Tech-savvy businesses that often overlook UX.
- Comic bookstores & collectible toy shops – Many are locally owned and could benefit from e-commerce improvements.
- Cosplay costume makers & fabricators – Many small creators sell online but need better user experience.

Do you love weddings?

The wedding industry is massive and many businesses have websites in need of UX and accessibility help:

- Florists – Online ordering for wedding arrangements should be easy and intuitive.
- Photographers & videographers – Many portfolio sites are visually heavy and lack proper structure.
- Wedding planners – These businesses rely on clear communication and scheduling, making UX critical.
- Event venues – Often have accessibility issues with booking and venue information.
- DJs and live music providers – Service packages should be clearly presented.
- Lighting & equipment rental companies – Many utilize confusing order forms.
- Event rentals (tables, chairs, décor, etc.) – UX improvements can simplify the rental process.

Are you a DIYer or love handmade goods?

Makers and artisans often don't have the time or skills to make their websites accessible:

- Woodworkers & furniture makers – Small businesses often have visually heavy but inaccessible sites.
- Jewelry designers & crafters – Many often sell through Instagram or Etsy but could benefit from a better site.
- Pottery studios & ceramic artists – Often rely on outdated gallery-style websites.
- Quilters & textile artists – Many have personal websites that could be improved for accessibility.
- 3D printing & custom fabrication services – Niche but growing and UX can help them scale.

Do you enjoy physical activities and sports?

Sports and recreation businesses often have websites that could benefit from better accessibility:

- Archery & sport shooting ranges – Booking and safety instructions need to be clear and accessible.
- Axe-throwing bars – A growing trend but many of their websites are hard to use.
- Escape rooms – Often have poorly designed booking and FAQ pages.
- Mini golf courses – Online reservations and event bookings could be improved.
- Bouncy house rentals – Parents need an easy, accessible way to book inflatables.
- Skating rinks – Ticket sales and event scheduling can be confusing without proper UX.

Do you love traveling or exploring?

Businesses in tourism and hospitality often have major accessibility gaps.

- Bed & breakfasts & boutique hotels – Many don't even have mobile-friendly sites.
- Guided tour companies – Whether city tours or hiking excursions, UX can make or break bookings.
- RV rental businesses – Online booking systems can be difficult for users with disabilities.

- Local adventure companies (kayaking, zip-lining, rock climbing) – Many have DIY websites with accessibility barriers.
- Travel planners & agencies – Many serve niche markets but have outdated digital experiences.

Many businesses exist because someone had an idea or a skill they could offer in exchange for money. Your job is to identify a few topics you have knowledge about and start connecting the dots to find adjacent opportunities. As for the horseback riding lessons, I found a company I was excited to work with, and I have been taking weekly riding lessons. Every single website I found during my search also went on my potential client tracker.

Focus on What You Already Know

Another option to find potential clients is to pick a topic that you have knowledge of, something that you'd be excited about growing more expertise in. Choosing a topic you already have an interest in makes it easier to work with the business owners not only because you're already excited about the product or service and have an understanding of it but also because you already have knowledge of the user experience. For instance, if you've taken martial arts lessons since your childhood, you might be interested in looking at different martial arts company websites, which you will have used before as a customer. If you are an avid knitter, you might look at knitting shops and pattern websites, places where you can purchase yarn, or even small producers that develop their own yarn blends. Maybe even look at alpaca farm websites or other related industry suppliers.

When I was 20, I worked as a receptionist and service manager for a family-owned plumbing company. I know enough about the industry still that I can empathize and "speak the same industry language" as the folks who own plumbing companies. They would be an ideal client for me to reach out to; there is a surprising number of plumbing companies that exist in my area. Similarly, that opens up the idea of working with other home service businesses, such as a drain cleaning service or HVAC companies. What other services can you think of that a homeowner might require? Any topic idea you have can provide numerous potential customers. What jobs have you had or become aware of as a result of your parents, friends, or family members working in them? What context-related websites can you come up with?

Take action by sitting down to do a brainstorm. Set a timer and focus your efforts on considering how every part of your chosen topic comes to be realized. Maybe you have an interest in winemaking or wine tasting. You could look at winery websites. You could look at farms that provide grapes to wineries. You could look at food services that provide picnic snacks to local wineries. You could look at an organization that hosts "dinner in the field" events at wineries around a particular area. You could even look at logistics companies that provide shipping for wine or transport for local events. There are endless opportunities to find topic-adjacent businesses that we hadn't previously thought of simply because we have not explored related businesses. The possibilities are endless, especially once you start taking a more holistic view of a topic you are passionate or knowledgeable about.

This way of finding websites that you can work with also gives you an advantage over your potential competitors. Just as people can detect someone's boredom or lack of interest in a topic or conversation, they can also sense enthusiasm and excitement. By finding a business that has a relationship to things you're excited about, you will naturally be more engaged in those projects. These business owners will in turn feel and share your excitement to work together.

START LOCAL

One of my favorite ways to find small businesses to work with is by looking for what exists near me. Open Google Maps and zoom in on your area. If you are in a very rural area, you may have to slide the map around quite a lot. What you're looking for, however, are businesses that you may never have heard of, because you have simply not needed their services. If you're in a suburban area, you might even see that there are businesses registered at houses near you. In my suburban area, there are many interesting businesses that do not have traditional storefronts, but they are official businesses with real clients and income. In my neighborhood there is a service plumbing company, a tailor, a tax preparer, and a property manager. You will be surprised at the number of businesses that you've never heard of simply because you haven't seen their name on a sign outside their business.

Find Hidden Businesses Near You

Many small businesses are hidden away in small clusters of buildings or in what we call "strip malls," a long building housing multiple storefronts. We often don't notice them because we have no reason to visit the area, or they're on the way to somewhere else and you've never looked over while driving to see what the business is. On Google Maps, they are labeled and their website is usually attached to their profile. As you're scrolling through the Google Maps page, zoom in until you're essentially looking at a couple of buildings that take up the space of your computer screen. Take a moment to notice all the different companies that are listed within a small area. Open up at least 10 of these websites. Simply right click on the website link and open it in a new tab until you have at least 10 of these business websites open.

Start looking at each of the websites. Even at your level, without being able to instantly spot accessibility issues, you can make a judgment on whether or not the website needs some work. Add these companies to your potential client outreach list, without prejudging the website, your own skills, or the business. Remember, the goal is just to make a list of people you can potentially reach out to.

Build Personal Relationships by Connecting in Person

There is one thing that can make working with these local businesses happen more quickly than just adding them to your potential client outreach tracker in preparation for the next chapter. The action is simple: stop in and say "hello." Initiate the process by dropping by a small business in person as you are out and about running your errands and living your day-to-day life. If you take notice of a small business, perhaps a dry-cleaning business or an independent beauty shop, stop in and say "hello." The first principles of marketing tell us that people love doing business with other people that they know, like, and trust. Introducing yourself, making eye contact, and shaking hands with another human are incredibly valuable practices for building that "know, like, and trust" factor with complete strangers. One of the best benefits gained from connecting in person is that even if they don't need your services, they are happy to recommend someone they know who does.

Between finding companies that you have an interest in and companies in your physical proximity, you should be able to create a good-sized list of potential clients you can reach out to. Now, let's talk about one more way to find a local client before we start the outreach process.

Who Do You Know?

Do not underestimate the power of personal referrals. I worry that this last suggestion is too simple, but I would be remiss if I didn't mention it. There are two ways I suggest getting personal referrals to small businesses that you can work with at your level:

- People in your immediate and secondary circles
- People your immediate and secondary circles can introduce you to

In the supplementary materials of this book, you'll find a document called The Memory Jogger. This is a variation of a document found easily online through a number of multi-level marketing or direct marketing websites. It is a comprehensive list meant to jog your memory about the people in your network. The network in this instance isn't just the professional connections you have on LinkedIn, but rather the interconnected group of individuals you know through every aspect of your life.

Most people when asked "Do you know anybody...?" can only come up with a handful of names. These are typically the most recent interactions they have had, or the people they are closest to. Your true network, though, is much, much larger.

The first group of people, your immediate circle, is the folks you interact with regularly: your parents, siblings, aunts, uncles, grandparents, and maybe even your cousins. Your immediate circle might include close friends or even coworkers.

Do any of these people have a business they are building? A hobby they are monetizing? A service they provide to friends and neighbors? If they have a website, they are a candidate for your services. Add to your potential client outreach tracker anyone who has a small business or is a sole entrepreneur (often referred to as a "solopreneur"). If you're not sure whether they have a business, ask. Lead with curiosity and find out more about what they're doing. They will be excited to tell you about it, and you might find a potential customer. Many students have landed their first client through a family member or close friend.

The second group of people, your secondary circle, is the people you spend time around occasionally: your hairdresser, landscaper, tax preparer, casual photographer friend, or folks at your kid's soccer camp or in your tennis club. This circle might include your mentors, neighbors, and members of a social circle, such as your church, mosque, synagogue, or temple. Start making a list of all these people you are loosely connected to. If you're not sure, put them on the list anyway.

Once you start creating the list of people you might reach out to, you'll discover that your list is much longer than you expected. This happens to every single student who starts creating the list, and it will happen to you. As you start to empty your mind of the people you know, your brain will start to identify even more connections. Once you start thinking about your best friends, you will start to think about all of the people in their inner circle who might be potential clients. Every organization you've ever been a part of, everything you've ever done, holds an opportunity for landing a first-project client.

Any one of these people—and likely many of them—could have a website for their service- or product-based business and need what you are offering.

Who Do They Know?

Even if your connections do not need your services immediately, you should ask a simple question: "Who do you know that I should know?" This question works to jog *their* memory for potential clients they can introduce you to. Think about your family; who do they know? What about your friends; who do they know? Think about all of the relationships in your life and the circles they interact with. These are all potential future customers.

The key thing to remember when reviewing the memory jogger is that you're not selling these people something. You're just asking, "Hey, I am looking for my first client for a Website Accessibility and Usability Evaluation. Do you know anyone who has a small website?" While the memory jogger concept comes from network marketing, that's not what we're doing here. We are just gathering a list of people we might be able to help through an accessibility-focused website evaluation that can protect them from lawsuits.

By the time you work through the entire memory jogger document, you will have at least a handful of people you can reach out to. Ideally, you should have a list of about 20 potential opportunities before moving to the next chapter, where we will create an outreach plan and start making contact with potential clients.

How to Approach the Business

Now that we have a list of a few potential customers we think we want to work with, let us come up with a plan for how we are going to approach them. Often, this is the part where people begin to feel nervous. If there is one thing you take from this chapter, however, it should be the knowledge that you have the ability to do this. Being able to approach people and introduce yourself is not a skill unique to a few individuals, but something that each one of us has the ability to develop. The only way we can grow this skill is through practice. It becomes much easier to practice through preparation and knowing what you are going to say.

In this chapter, we will discuss the types of goals small businesses set, what business metrics they may assess, and what to look for when taking a first look at a business website. We will also talk about communicating what you do and the value you can bring to the owners of a small business.

UNDERSTANDING SMALL BUSINESS GOALS

Have you ever considered what is required for a company to stay in business? "Money" might be your first response, and you would be absolutely correct with that answer. There are, however, many other factors that are at play. In order to get money, or "generate revenue," a business needs customers. Every business needs customers who are willing to trade their money for that business's services or goods. Even without deep knowledge about each business, we can make an educated guess about what kind of customers they need.

What Kind of Customers Small Businesses Need

A salon needs customers who want hair cutting and styling, eyebrow or body waxing, manicures and pedicures, and facials and massages. A restaurant needs customers who want to experience delicious food. A bar and music venue needs customers who want to have a good time with a crowd listening to a band or musicians. A craft store needs customers who are interested in buying supplies such as paint, beads, and picture frames. A daycare center needs parents who are looking for regular childcare. A dance center needs students who are interested in taking classes such as ballet, tap dancing, and salsa dancing. Travel agencies need customers who want to travel. Storage services need customers who need to free up room in their house or garage.

If you find a business and you are unable to immediately identify the types of customers they need, do a quick search online. Consider asking ChatGPT, for example, "What kinds of people use a notary public service business?" In fact, give it a shot right now. Maybe you have never needed the services of a notary. You will find that there are many reasons a person might need a notary: people buying a house require their mortgage documents, deeds, and closing papers to be notarized to verify their authenticity. People making a will require their final words and wishes to be notarized to be recognized legally. Parents with minor children may need to notarize travel documents or medical consent forms. Notary public services are often required for immigration, travel, adoption, marriage, legal agreements, financial records, and more.

The point to take away from this brief search exercise is this: everything is "figureoutable" if we take a couple of additional steps to learn more. None of this information is secret or hidden, and it is always a good idea to get a sense of to whom a small business might be marketing their products and services. This will enable you to refine your approach to that small business in a way that makes them more likely to do business with *you*.

Likely Goals for Small Businesses

Once we have a good idea of the types of customers a small business needs, we can start to identify its likely goals. Typically, small business goals can be broken down into two things: make more money and reduce the cost of serving existing customers. Making more money can be done in a few ways, but most frequently, this is done by gaining new customers or selling existing customers more services and products.

You are not expected to be a sales or marketing expert or know the ins and outs of business development for every type of business. So remember, everything is figureoutable. If we ask ChatGPT, "What are some ways a tax preparation business's website can help it meet business goals?" we learn several interesting things.

The website for a tax preparation business might be trying to attract new customers, which improves the business by bringing in more money. The website could also help expand awareness of additional services such as bookkeeping and financial planning with the intention of increasing the amount each customer spends. Both of these goals increase the amount of money the tax service business can make. The website could help streamline onboarding operations by integrating with a calendar service to allow new customers to self-book appointments or fill out the necessary paperwork, which reduces the cost of providing the service to existing customers. Almost every business metric, however it is worded, can be broken down to meet these two goals. This is an extreme simplification of how business goals are set and measured. Hopefully, you can see how this plays into your work and the value you can provide to a small business.

Quickly Assessing Success Metrics

Regardless of your level of business knowledge and professional experience, you have the ability to make a quick assessment of how well a website is supporting business goals. Let's take a look at a real example. Open up a new tab in your web browser and search for orthodontist near me. Then, click on any of the non-ad options that show up. It doesn't matter whether you find the company through Google Maps or through a search engine; just open up the website for the closest orthodontist to you. For reference, here are some potential business goals an orthodontic provider might have for their website:

- Attracting new patients (making more money)
- Advertising new services (making more money)
- Offering a payment portal (reducing the cost of serving existing patients)
- Providing online forms (reducing the cost of serving existing patients)
- Showing testimonials and reviews (attracting new patients = more money)

How do you think the business is doing at meeting those goals? If you think you are not qualified to make a judgment about this website, that is simply not true. As a consumer, you already have the gut instinct needed to make a general assessment. Even as a new designer, freshly graduated from a design bootcamp, you have the ability to make this snap judgment.

Imagine yourself as a potential new customer visiting the website. Is the website visually pleasing? Do you feel like you would be interested in working with this orthodontist if you needed their services? Does the website feel like it is easy to navigate, or is it difficult to find information about the orthodontist and team? Is the information about their services provided in a clear and understandable format? How easy is it to find the hours of operation and other contact information? Do you notice a patient portal where existing patients can log in to make payments or schedule appointments? Are online forms readily available? Do you see testimonials from former patients who are happy with their orthodontic treatment? Are reviews provided through online services such as Google or Trustpilot? All of these details are discoverable within the first 60 seconds of looking at a website.

Any time you take a look at the website for a potential client, you can search for the basic goals the business might have and make an educated guess at how well the website is supporting those goals. Practice doing this "quick assessment" for every potential customer on your outreach tracking spreadsheet. As you continue to get to know small businesses and what their goals might be, you will get better at making these assessments about their potential success.

The First Impression

First impressions are crucial because they shape how people perceive value and make decisions, both consciously and subconsciously. Our brains instinctively process initial cues to evaluate trustworthiness, competence, and likability, and these early assessments set the tone for subsequent interactions. This phenomenon, known as the primacy effect, refers to the cognitive bias that prioritizes the first information we encounter, making it more likely to influence memory and decision-making. (6) In a business context, the primacy effect highlights why a customer's first experience with a business often determines their willingness to engage further, including whether they choose to spend money.

When you first visit a website, take notice of your first emotional reaction. If your initial reaction is closer to the grimacing emoji than the grinning emoji, it is likely that many others feel the same way. Is there anything off-putting or that needs improvement? Even if you cannot name something specific, if it feels odd, odds are good that other new customers get the same sense.

Head back to your favorite search engine and look for an HVAC business near you. Take a look at their website. How does it make you feel about the business? Do the services and business owners seem trustworthy? Do the products they use appear to be of high quality and desirable? How credible is this business? For you as a consumer, how does it feel to think about giving them your hard-earned money in exchange for their service? If the website is not giving you a sense of confidence, the business is likely a good candidate for you to reach out to.

COMMUNICATING THE VALUE YOU BRING

Something to keep in mind regarding these small business websites is that an entrepreneur or small business owner does not know everything. There are few requirements for starting a business, and being an entrepreneur does not mean they have a business degree. Even businesses run by people with Masters degrees in Business Administration "don't know what they don't know." They cannot possibly know everything about everything. They know their realm, and we know our realm. That is why we can bring value to their business.

Approach with Empathy

Empathy is a core tenet for designers for a reason. We want to be part of a rising tide that lifts all boats. Since small business owners have little exposure to our world of UX design, we must approach them with empathy. We want these businesses to be successful, because successful small businesses are the backbone of a healthy economy. When small business owners are successful, they work with other small businesses and individuals in the area, passing around money and increasing financial prosperity in the community. We want to encourage that and empower them, and how we approach them to sell our services greatly matters. Small business owners have likely created their own website with the best of intentions, yet are often unaware when their website is providing a poor user experience. Telling a business owner that their website is ugly is just about the same as telling a new mom their baby is ugly. It does not foster a positive experience and is likely to shut down the conversation entirely.

Remember, we are selling a service that will enhance the website experience for all customers. Instead of focusing on a website's aesthetics, we will have far more success appealing to their sense of community and empathy and their business acumen. We can accomplish this by helping them understand why accessibility matters.

Communicating the Value of an Accessible Website

Unlike our potential customers, we know that accessibility is increasingly important. It is also safe to assume that they are unaware that website related digital accessibility lawsuits are on the rise. In 2022 over 2,200 digital accessibility lawsuits were filed in the United States. In 2023, this number more than doubled with over 4,600 digital accessibility lawsuits filed. (7) Interestingly, e-commerce websites in particular were the targets of 82% of digital accessibility lawsuits filed in 2023. Furthermore, smaller companies, those generating less than $25 million in yearly revenue, account for 73% of digital accessibility lawsuits. (9) It is also worth noting that while larger companies that often face legal action have started to proactively invest in manual website accessibility audits and remediation, small businesses typically only address accessibility issues after being targeted with an Americans with Disabilities Act of 1990 (ADA) demand letter or being sued.

Since small business owners typically have no awareness of the legal requirements regarding website accessibility, nor that they can potentially be targeted by digital accessibility lawsuits, it is our job to help them understand what accessibility is and why it matters. An excellent way to describe accessibility to an entrepreneur or small business owner is this: accessibility is making sure that our customers can perceive, understand, navigate, and interact with our websites. Accessibility matters because, in many cases, it is legally required, but also because it is a good business practice. Many people believe it is also, ultimately, the right thing to do.

So what is the value of an accessible website? How can a small business owner be convinced that caring about the accessibility of their website matters? As we discussed earlier in this chapter, small business goals typically focus on two things: making more money and spending less money to deliver their goods and services. Here are some ways to talk about making more money and saving money by having an accessible website.

Making Money

Users with disabilities make up a market the size of China. 1.3 billion people in the world (16% of all humans) are living with one or more disabilities, and they have money to spend just like people without disabilities. Having an accessible website expands the market a business can target. If a company can sell more products or services to more people, that is a good thing.

There is no demographic for disability. Every user demographic has disabled people. A small business cannot say that "none of our users have disabilities" because there is no way to know that this is true. Users with disabilities cannot be segmented out of our marketing efforts, meaning we cannot avoid marketing to people living with disabilities.

Saving Money

Save money by avoiding legal costs. Conducting a Website Accessibility and Usability Evaluation can help protect small businesses from spending $25,000 or more after facing a digital accessibility lawsuit in the United States. While $25,000 is an average settlement, it is by no means the maximum cost—some lawsuits result in six-figure settlements or court-ordered remediation that forces businesses to spend far more than they would have if they had addressed accessibility proactively.

Additionally, businesses that have settled a digital accessibility lawsuit are more likely to be targeted by additional lawsuits. Once a company is on the radar of accessibility law firms, it often becomes a repeat target, making proactive accessibility improvements not just an ethical or legal consideration but a critical risk-reduction strategy.

Reducing Spending

Reduce business spending by driving fewer customer service calls and emails. An inaccessible website means more frustrated customers who can't complete their purchases, find the information they need, or successfully book services. When users struggle with poor UX or inaccessible interfaces, they don't just give up—they reach out for help.

Every customer service phone call, email, or chat message requesting assistance comes with a cost. A small business might not track these costs, but consider:

- Every minute spent answering the same questions (e.g., "How do I book an appointment?" or "Where can I find your pricing?") is a minute that could have been spent on higher-value tasks.
- If multiple people are reaching out with the same issue, that's a systemic problem—not just a one-off request.

- Many businesses lose customers without even realizing it because those who encounter accessibility barriers simply leave the site without reaching out.

By making their website accessible, small business owners can reduce time spent on avoidable customer service interactions, allowing them to focus on delivering their products and services instead of troubleshooting their website.

Reduce spending by providing fewer refunds and dealing with chargebacks. An inaccessible checkout process or service booking system can cause accidental purchases, duplicate charges, or incomplete transactions, leading to:

- More refund requests, adding manual administrative work.
- Chargebacks (which come with fees from credit card processors).
- Lost sales if frustrated users abandon the purchase rather than call for help.

Accessible websites ensure that all customers can successfully complete transactions the first time, reducing unnecessary refund and chargeback costs.

Reduce spending on unnecessary marketing. Many small businesses invest in SEO, social media ads, and paid marketing to drive traffic to their website. But what good is paying for traffic if users can't complete a purchase or sign up?

If 16% of all potential customers (those with disabilities) find the site difficult or impossible to use, that's wasted marketing spend. By making their website accessible, small business owners can ensure they convert more visitors into paying customers, getting more value from their marketing efforts.

GETTING COMFORTABLE TALKING ABOUT WHAT YOU DO

These Website Accessibility and Usability Evaluations are valuable to conduct, regardless of your level of experience. You are applying your existing level of expertise and knowledge to help improve business metrics in measurable ways. As you get your first real-world experience, it is especially important to remember *not* to undersell yourself. Your level of knowledge, even just a few months out of a technical bootcamp, is more than that of the business owner when it comes to understanding the accessibility of websites. Be confident when describing what you know, and do not add doubt to the mind of the entrepreneur or small business owner you are speaking to by downplaying your capabilities. How do you get more comfortable talking about what you do? Describe it clearly, follow a script, and practice until you are proficient. In the resources for this book, you will find a document titled Website Evaluation Script that contains:

- The basic script
- Reasons why small business owners should care about accessibility
- Details regarding a few disabilities and how many people have them
- Additional script details you might include

Use these resources to craft and refine your pitch as you approach potential clients.

Describe What You Do

To be super clear: by following the process this book is teaching, you are an early-career designer or developer, a career-changer, a website designer, etc., and you are looking for real-world, industry-recognized experience. To gain this experience, you are offering a Website Accessibility and Usability Evaluation to a small business to help them identify the accessibility barriers that typically trigger digital accessibility lawsuits. It does not need to be more complicated than that. The more you add to the introduction, the more chances you give a person to tune out and ignore you. Do not feel like you need to add more words to sound impressive, or to take up more space. Keep it simple and clear.

Miller's Law is the psychological principle that states that the average person can hold about seven items in their working memory, give or take a few things. (9) Translated to the real world: we must remember that people have a lot going on at any one time. Not only are they listening to your pitch, but they are also thinking of their to-do list, they are wondering whether they turned the oven off this morning, they are reminding themselves to pick up milk before they go home, and they just realized they poured a cup of tea and forgot to drink it. An overly detailed pitch means overwhelming information and cognitive overload for the listener. The more overwhelmed people feel, the less smart they feel. The less smart they feel, the more likely they are to say "no." Make it easy for them to say "yes" to you.

Follow a Script

When you are just starting out offering this website evaluation to get real-world experience, it is crucial that you follow a script. Without a script, you are setting yourself up to stumble over your tongue, forget your name, and struggle to pull together a cohesive sentence.

Here is a basic script, written from my perspective: "My name is Maigen Thomas, and I'm a freelance website designer. I offer website evaluations to help small businesses identify issues that typically lead to expensive digital accessibility lawsuits. Are you the person in charge of digital accessibility compliance for your company's website?"

The person you are speaking to will confirm that they are the person in charge of the website, or they will direct you to the person who is in charge of the website. Or they will ask what you mean. What you say next will depend on the level of interest they show in digital accessibility or website design, or in understanding the context of your pitch a little better. The details in this book regarding accessibility should help you answer most of their questions.

All of these are openings for you to provide a little bit more detail and bring them along with you. This is your opportunity to talk about how digital accessibility impacts users and how many people in the world live with disabilities.

Notice that the script uses plain language and does not overwhelm the person you are speaking to with technical terms or industry jargon. This is on purpose and follows a variation of Skunk Works' Kelly Johnson's originally coined line, the KISS method: Keep It Super SImple. Remember, make it easy for them to say "yes" to you!

Practice Makes Proficient

Practice your script! Practice makes you proficient. It does not make you perfect. You will never be perfect. There is no such thing as perfect; perfection does not exist. Stop trying to reach for perfection and just keep practicing.

Practice it 100 times. Okay, maybe 100 repetitions seems like a lot (and it is), but practice delivering your pitch as many times as you can. Practice will not make your sales pitch perfect, but it will make it easier to deliver. Practice this script with your best friend, your parents, your siblings, your romantic partner, your dog, and your mail delivery person. Practice it on the barista you talk to the next time you get coffee.

Practice it with anyone who will let you, because practice makes it easier to perform when it really matters. You will get a sense of whether your pitch is too long, not compelling, or confusing. You *will* flub this a few times, so expect that, accept it, and keep going. You will likely refine this pitch at least a dozen times as you get more comfortable explaining what you do and why it matters.

In the next chapter, we are going to work on how to sell your service: how to ask for the sale, and what to go for instead of an immediate "yes"—it is not what you think!

CHAPTER 3

Sell Your Service

In this chapter, we'll talk about how to sell your services, what benefits a website assessment can provide for a small business, and why the process is so valuable that small business owners will say "yes" almost immediately. We'll also talk about the mindset you need for outreach and dealing with rejection. By the end of this chapter, you will be able to confidently approach a business owner about your services, follow a script and ask for the sale, and handle rejection gracefully while not taking it personally. We will start with a brief introduction to why sales is a necessary skill.

INTRODUCTION TO SELLING

Selling is a skill that early-career digital technologists often struggle with. To be fair, most people struggle with selling as a soft skill. Many people assume if they are not in a sales role, they do not need to learn how to sell. That could not be further from the truth.

There can be a lot of discomfort around sales and discussions of money, in large part because of how often selling is associated with self-promotion and financial negotiations. Developing the ability to sell your services is not just beneficial, however—it is utterly essential for your career growth. This section aims to ease your anxiety about approaching a potential customer and asking for money in exchange for your services. This section will also help you cultivate a positive mindset toward selling as a soft skill. Getting comfortable with selling is key. Once you are used to asking for a sale, following a script, and handling rejection gracefully, you will truly be able to accomplish anything in your career.

Understanding the Importance of Selling

Without sales, there is no economy. Sales, in a way, makes the world go 'round. As your career progresses, you will find yourself selling more often than you ever thought possible. In fact, your job isn't just to deliver great work; it's to convince your clients and coworkers of the value you bring.

Regardless of your job role, the ability to sell is essential. For the rest of your career, you will be selling your ideas, your products, your services, and your abilities. For career advancement, you will need to convince stakeholders and managers that your design choices are the right direction. You will sell them on the value of your work and suggestions. Selling your ideas effectively can lead to greater influence within your organization and more impactful outcomes for users and the business. If you decide to go freelance or become a consultant, your livelihood will depend on your ability to attract and retain clients. For now, we can take a look at getting into a sales mindset.

Getting into a Sales Mindset

The sales process can feel uncomfortable at first, especially when asking for money, but it's a critical skill to develop. Feeling anxious about selling is natural. To help calm your mind about selling and develop a more comfortable and confident approach, consider these things:

1. Selling is helping. Shift your perspective away from thinking of selling as a self-serving activity; think of it as an activity where you are offering valuable assistance. Your goal is to help clients improve their websites, which ultimately benefits their business. Accessible websites ensure users of all levels of ability can access the goods and services they need.

2. Adopt a growth mindset. Recognize that selling is not an innate talent but a skill that can be improved over time with persistent effort and practice. Each interaction, whether successful or not, is an opportunity for you to learn and grow. By continually seeking to understand what worked and what did not, you can make incremental improvements that lead to greater proficiency and more success. Like a baseball player, you can measure your improvement over time simply by getting more opportunities to practice. Approaching this skill with a growth mindset will not only enhance your ability to sell but also foster resilience and adaptability, two essential traits for long-term success in this or any career.

3. Embrace authenticity. Authenticity builds trust. Rather than trying to adopt a style similar to sales approaches that may have felt unappealing in the past, focus on having genuine conversations. Be yourself and let your passion for helping people and businesses shine through.

Keep this in mind and you will gain the confidence you need to market yourself and your skills effectively. Now that you have nudged your mindset toward this shift and started building the confidence to sell your services, we can look at what exactly you are selling.

WHAT YOU ARE SELLING

In the next chapter, we will get into the details of how to conduct a website evaluation; but first, it is important to be clear about what, exactly, you are selling. Knowing that what you are selling brings value to customers will help you build confidence in this process.

You are selling a low-cost, high-value website assessment that checks for accessibility and usability issues that can prevent users from purchasing goods and services. Your evaluation will provide small businesses with feedback and actionable insights that they can use immediately to improve the experience users have on their website. Additionally, these improvements can positively impact website performance and legal compliance, protecting the business owner's interests.

Why Offer a Website Evaluation for $100?

This book suggests that you price your first evaluation at just $100. The cost of this service is deliberately low. Pricing a valuable service so low makes it an easy decision for a small business owner to agree to it, allowing them to test the value you bring with minimal financial risk. Remember, your ultimate goal is to get real-world, industry-recognized experience at a time when early-career digital technologists are not getting career traction. Your role is to communicate that this evaluation delivers way more value than what they are paying for.

Not only is the price low enough to make it easy for a small business owner to say an enthusiastic "yes!" but it is also a low enough price to help you feel comfortable asking for money in exchange for your knowledge and abilities. This service is just a foot in the door: a way to demonstrate your skills, build relationships, and potentially open the door further to future, higher-value work. We will talk about how to present yourself to do that future, higher-value work in a later chapter. For now, offering this valuable service at a low cost is a crucial practice in overcoming the hesitation to ask for money.

What Makes This an Easy Yes

Small business owners generally find it hard to say "no" to this offer due to the high value for the low price. Getting actionable insights that they can use to improve the revenue of their business for this price is unheard of. While these business owners might balk at hiring an early-career or "junior" person on a part-time or full-time basis, this level of investment is both low risk and high reward for business owners. The price tag makes it easy to say "yes" to. The results you deliver after the evaluation will demonstrate your ability to deliver work above and beyond what they might expect. Remember, you are more of an expert than they are, in this area at least.

Your job in selling this service is to make it clear that you will address issues that could affect their website's usability and conversion rate. The "conversion rate" is the rate at which website visitors become paying customers. People who can't perceive, understand, or operate a website are not likely to become paying customers.

The $100 price tag is a small investment to get professional feedback on:

- *Accessibility*: Can people of all ability levels use the website?
- *Usability*: Can new users easily understand the website?
- *Information Architecture*: Is the website easy to navigate?
- *Visual Design*: Does the website look inviting and aesthetically pleasing?
- *Content Readability*: Is the website content clear and understandable?

You can frame this service as a way to demonstrate your abilities and expertise with low risk on the part of the business owner. This allows you to revisit the conversation after the initial evaluation and offer your website design and development skills at a fair rate. This evaluation is a chance for them to improve their business outcomes while you gain experience and a case study for your portfolio, ultimately advancing your career. Since this evaluation does much more than assess the aesthetics of a website, it can provide feedback that directly improves business outcomes. The $100 price point minimizes financial friction for small business owners, making the decision straightforward. Now that you see the value in offering this service at a low cost (at first), we can talk about how to ask for the sale.

HOW TO ASK FOR THE SALE

We have discussed how important it is to sell your service, but how do you go about actually selling it? Now, we will review how to land the sale.

Be Honest About Your Experience Level

No matter where you are in your career, you can provide value to a business owner. You have knowledge, experience, and insight that the business owner does not have. Contrary to some advice found online, there is no need to claim you have more experience in your career than you actually do. You have not spent 10, 20, or 30 years in the industry, but that just means you have a fresh perspective, unburdened by a long history of "how you have always done it."

Similarly, do not downplay what you have done or how you have learned your skills. Even if your experience has been through a bootcamp or earned as a result of teaching yourself, this is still relevant to the task. You might feel overwhelmed by the amount of information learned in a short period of time, and that is okay. You still have more experience, exposure, and knowledge in the areas of UX design, accessibility, and usability than the person you are pitching your offering to.

Remember that transparency builds trust. It may be appropriate to be upfront about being an early-career freelancer and that you are using this practice to build up your portfolio. This is a great explanation for business owners who appear wary of trusting a deal that seems "too good to be true," such as a website evaluation for just $100. Simply explain that building your portfolio is essential for landing the roles you want to get later in your career, and that is why they are getting such a great offer at such a low price.

Use Plain Language, Not Industry Jargon

No matter what kind of small business you are approaching, keep in mind that all parties in the conversation have an area of expertise. Speak in terms they can understand easily. Using plain language ensures that even the least tech-savvy business owner can understand what you are talking about. This is not the time to impress with all of the terms and methods you know. Speak at a level your grandparents could understand.

Keep in mind that it does not impress people when you speak over their heads, at a higher level than they understand. In fact, it makes selling your service more difficult. We do not want to make our potential clients feel stupid, which is what happens when we describe what we do using industry jargon and technical language. People are far less inclined to buy from other people who make them feel stupid.

Think back to a time you picked up an object of interest at a shop you were visiting. If you could not immediately understand what the object was and why you needed it, you would set it back down. The same is true for a service, no matter how valuable it might be to the business owner. If they do not immediately understand why it is important and how it fits their needs, it is not worth their time or money even if it is at a low price. By speaking at a level anyone can understand, we make it easy for the business owner to trust us and say "yes."

The Most Effective Communication Channels

To actually speak to someone with the authority to say "yes" to your offer, you need to meet them where they are. Depending on your level of comfort and experience striking up conversations with strangers, there are several ways to do this. Approach your potential client with the method that works best for you, but keep in mind that some approaches are more effective than others. The following list is ordered from least effective to most effective.

Contact Form

The contact form on a business website is the least likely avenue to getting in front of a potential client and getting a "yes" response. There is no way to know ahead of time whether the contact form is even connected properly—what if your message never lands in their inbox? It is also the most ignorable outreach, because it is the most passive. It requires so little effort on your part that if you are not a paying customer, you likely will not get a response. It is just too easy for the company to ignore and put off a response, especially since you are reaching out to sell them something they are not yet convinced that they need.

Email

Sending an email is often the first outreach attempt practitioners of this process will try. It is an easy way to connect with someone you do not yet know. Similar to sending a message through the contact form of a website, this method of outreach has a low barrier of effort. Also, like the contact form outreach, it can be easily ignored once received. Think about how many emails you have received that you have not responded to because they are non-urgent or you need more time to think about how to reply. How many of those emails have simply fallen off the first page of your inbox? Now think about the experience of a small business owner that is a team of one or perhaps managing a few employees. Imagine the sheer amount of items in their inbox or on their to-do list. No matter how urgent-sounding your email subject line is, without good reason, the business owner may not prioritize getting back to you over the hundreds of must-do tasks they need to take care of first.

Remember, too, that these small business owners are more likely than not to have lower tech-savviness. They don't spend all of their waking time online. In my conversations, many business owners have admitted to me that they rarely check their email. In some cases, it was as rare as once a month!

Phone

If you want to get their attention, call the phone number on the website. Picking up the phone and making a call might seem old-fashioned if you are in one of the generations of people born after 1980, but this is still an incredibly effective method of outreach. Even if you are someone who keeps their mobile phone in silent mode 100% of the time, you cannot assume that is true of a business. You are highly likely to get a potential customer on the phone if you just try calling them. It is entirely understandable if that feels a little scary, and you are not alone in that feeling. Practice what you will say, and practice making phone calls before trying to connect with a future client. Ask your best friends or a group of friends if they would be willing to let you practice calling them and having this conversation. Practice will always make you more proficient! You will get more comfortable as you continue to push yourself out of your comfort zone and keep making phone calls. It does get easier.

In Person

It is impossible to state how effective meeting in person and shaking their hand can be when it comes to building a relationship with a client. Generally speaking, the older the business owner is, the more likely they are to appreciate a firm handshake and being able to look you in the eye. Many business owners report being more likely to work with a service provider after meeting them in person. Call it old-fashioned, but this real-world human connection proves to be the most successful way to approach business owners. You might stop by a business on your way to an appointment. Practice your pitch with your personal trainer, your dentist, and the grocery store manager on your next visit.

It is important to be confident in yourself, regardless of your method of approach. If it does not make sense to stop by a business in person, consider which of these methods of outreach will be most likely to connect with the owner. Keep in mind what works for your personality type and confidence level and keep trying various ways until you find what works best for you.

How to Use Social Media to Connect with Small Business Owners

Some small business owners are active on social media, often using it to market their services, engage with customers, and build their brands. While cold emails and phone calls can be effective, reaching out through social media can feel more natural and less intrusive. Here's how to do it right:

Find the Right Businesses to Connect With

Not all small businesses are active on social media, but many use it for customer engagement and marketing. Look for:

- Local businesses that promote themselves actively online.
- Service-based businesses (gyms, salons, consultants, therapists) that rely on online bookings.
- E-commerce brands that drive traffic through Instagram, TikTok, or Facebook Shops.
- Businesses struggling with engagement (e.g., their website link is broken, hard to navigate, or missing entirely).

Engage First, Don't Sell Immediately

Instead of jumping straight into pitching, start by engaging with their content. This helps build trust and familiarity, so when you do reach out, you won't feel like a stranger.

- Like and comment on their posts with thoughtful insights.
- Share their content if relevant to your audience.
- Send a supportive DM (e.g., "I loved your post about [topic]—great insights on [industry].").

Slide Into the DMs (Professionally!)

Once you've engaged with a few posts, send a direct message that focuses on value rather than a hard sell. Example DM templates:

For a local business owner: *"Hey [name], I love what you're doing with [business name]! I checked out your website and noticed a few small tweaks that could make it even easier for customers to book with you. I offer website evaluations for small businesses like yours—would you be open to a quick chat about how to make your site work even better for you?"*

For an e-commerce brand: *"Hi [name], I came across your store and love your products! I noticed something on your site that might be causing customers to drop off before checkout—would you be open to a quick (free) tip that could help boost conversions?"*

This soft approach piques interest without pressuring them into a sale.

Use Instagram and TikTok Stories for Visibility

Many small business owners respond faster to story replies than cold DMs. If they post a story, here is a quick set of actions to take:

- React with a quick emoji (low-effort engagement).
- Reply with a compliment or question to start a conversation.
- If they post about website frustrations, jump in with a helpful suggestion.

Join Small Business Facebook & LinkedIn Groups

Facebook and LinkedIn groups are goldmines for networking. Join small business groups and answer questions about websites and UX, share useful content a couple of times a week, and connect with business owners looking for help. Engaging here establishes your expertise so business owners come to you when they need help.

Follow Up Without Being Pushy

If a business doesn't respond, don't take it personally. Try following up a week later with a new insight, or spend a few days engaging with their content before reaching out again. You can also send a quick "Just checking in!" message. Here's an example:

"Hey [name], just wanted to follow up in case you missed my message. I know you're busy, but I'd love to help make your website work better for your business—let me know if you'd like a quick look!"

No matter how you approach the business, or even what you say to them, there is one thing that is absolutely non-negotiable when it comes to landing a new customer: you must say the words or you will not make the sale. What words? Read on.

Say the Words

No matter what else you talk about during the conversation with your potential client, you must remember to say the words: "Would you like to buy this service?" You can phrase this any way you like, but there must be a question and it should require a "yes" or "no" answer. Practice saying the phrase you finalize as many times as possible. Ideally, you will practice asking this question until it stops making your shoulders creep up toward your ears.

Follow your script and keep it simple: "Hi, I'm Maigen Thomas. I'm a freelance website designer specializing in website evaluations. I am reaching out because I noticed a few areas on your website where some customers with disabilities might have trouble buying your products or services. I offer a low-cost, high-value website evaluation for $100, which returns actionable information you can use to improve your website's performance and conversion rate. Would you be interested in buying this service?"

Why is it important to say the words? Grant Cardone, an internationally recognized sales training consultant, would likely emphasize that "asking for the sale" is a critical step in closing deals. Here's how he might describe it:

1. *Control the Outcome*: If you do not ask for the sale, you are leaving the outcome of the conversation up to chance. By taking control and asking, you direct the conversation toward a clear decision.

2. *People Expect to Be Asked*: In all of Cardone's books, he emphasizes that this sales conversation is a "two-way street" and customers expect you to ask for their business. Not asking could make your potential client feel like you are not serious or that the deal is not that important to you.

3. *Demonstrate Confidence*: Asking for the sale demonstrates to the customer that you are confident in your service and the value you provide. If you do not ask, it can indicate a lack of belief in yourself and your skills.

4. *Get the Money*: Everything in sales leads up to this moment. If you do not ask, you will not get paid. The sale is where you turn effort into income. Asking for the sale is required for your success.

If asking for the customer's commitment to work with you feels scary, that is totally normal. Stay confident, and know that even if they say "no," you did a great job. You should expect to hear "no" when you first ask for the sale.

GO FOR "NO"

Not only should you expect to hear "no," but it is also a great idea to practice being told "no" to get comfortable hearing it. Not because it is a fun experience, but so you can learn that it does not cause you physical pain when you hear it. This is actually something that your brain will convince you is happening! (10) Being rejected will feel painful because the brain interprets rejection as a form of social threat; social rejection activates the same neural pathways as physical pain.

The first time you get rejected after asking a customer to buy your service does not feel good. You will feel a psychological response for certain, such as disappointment or anxiety. You might even feel a physiological one, which could be a sensation anywhere in your body. Physiological responses can range from a gentle blush pinking your cheeks to a sensation in your gut that you have just fallen through the floor. Your heart rate might increase, and you might start to sweat or even feel terribly cold suddenly. Some folks report feeling dizzy or nauseated. All of these are protective responses generated by your brain, intended to keep you safe from a perceived threat. The fight or flight response is activated by the perceived social rejection, which is totally normal.

Building resilience to rejection over time helps reduce the intensity of these uncomfortable feelings. So, how can you build resilience?

Expect Them to Say "No"

The first thing you can do to build resilience to rejection is to go into each situation with the understanding that "no" is a common response. Quite often, getting "no" for an answer simply means "not right now." Many people need time to process information or are not ready to make a decision at that moment. Always ask whether you can follow up or reconnect with them at a later time. If they say "yes" to following up with them, make sure to add that information to your Potential Client Outreach Tracker document and follow through with following up. Send them a polite email reminding them of who you are and what you discussed with them. Consider including some details about what your website evaluation service may uncover, but keep it simple, with no more than three examples.

Approach every conversation with the mindset that rejection is part of the process, and that each "no" brings you closer to getting a "yes." Every time you ask for a sale in this experiment, you are getting better at refining your approach and finding the right clients.

Set a Goal: 100 No's

One technique to reduce the fear of rejection is to train yourself to feel it less by experiencing it more. Set a goal to collect a certain number of rejections to build the resilience it takes to get comfortable with your role as a seller throughout your career. Most people take a lifetime to build up a comfort level with rejection, but this is one skill you can learn in a hurry. Like a baseball player: the more attempts you have "at bat," the more likely you are to get better at batting and hit more balls. It is nearly inevitable. If it terrifies you to even attempt this process, set a goal to get just 10 "no's." If you have enough moxie to shoot for a real challenge, try to pitch your service to 100 small business owners and learn from every "no" you hear.

There are so many benefits that you can gain from setting such a big, audacious goal. Setting a goal to make 100 attempts at talking to a small business owner and offering your services gives you the chance to gather valuable information and tweak your pitch along the way. Even with rejection, there is always something to learn from that feedback. This is a great opportunity to update your Potential Client Outreach Tracker with any feedback or notes about when to follow up. A goal of 100 attempts to reach out to sell a website evaluation in the next six months only means reaching out to five potential customers every week.

If you treat every "no" you hear as a chance to learn and adjust your approach, you will never reach that 100th "no." You will have already garnered enough enthusiastic "yes" clients to keep you busy. Also, you will have all but inoculated yourself against the emotional response to hearing the word "no" and will be, essentially, rejection proof.

HANDLING REJECTION GRACEFULLY

Just like getting better at asking for the sale comes with practice, so does handling rejection gracefully. The more you practice your pitch and receive feedback, the more confident and comfortable you will become and the easier it will be to recognize that rejection is merely redirection. It is almost never an outright, direct rejection. As Jia Jiang mentions in his TED talk, *What I learned from 100 days of rejection*, "Rejection is rarely personal. Most of the time, rejection has little to do with you, and everything to do with the situation." Every rejection has a reason, or even many reasons, behind it. The reasons are often complex and stem from factors we are not aware of. This should help you understand that "no" is rarely personal. (11)

Learning how to receive rejection with maturity and curiosity can often lead to future success. Jiang says: "A 'no' is not the end, but often the beginning of a deeper conversation." Not getting an immediate positive response provides an opportunity to explore further, understand the reasons why, or find alternatives. The response could turn into a "yes" with a different approach, better timing, or a slightly different offer.

Rejection, often perceived as a setback, can become a pivotal opportunity for personal and professional growth when approached with grace. By reacting calmly and thoughtfully, it's possible to turn a definitive "no" into a "not yet" or even open the door to a future "yes." Remaining curious and open-minded, asking for feedback, and genuinely listening to responses can turn up insights we might otherwise have missed. This is powerful personal development, and it demonstrates respect and professionalism—essential for leaving a positive impression.

You can take this professionalism a step further and express gratitude for the opportunity, even when faced with rejection. This kind of response to rejection fosters goodwill and respect from potential customers, differentiating you from potential competition and creating the beginning of a lasting, fruitful relationship. Ultimately, the true measure of our character lies not in how we handle success, but in our response to rejection. By making the mindset shift to understanding that rejection is simply part of an ongoing dialogue, we build resilience and poise and set ourselves up for even more success in the future.

How to Overcome Objections and Ask Again

In the case that the potential customer doesn't give a firm "no" and has one of the following responses, you can attempt to overcome the first "no" with some gentle pushback. Some business owners might just be hesitant or unsure about the need for a website evaluation. Here are some common objections and a brief response to potentially overcome them:

"Our website is fine."

The business owner might mention a recent redesign, or that they feel confident that the website is already meeting their needs. In that case, your response could be to explain that even visually appealing websites can have underlying usability or accessibility issues that are turning away potential customers. You might mention that about 15% of the population is living with a disability. You might explain that some very common accessibility issues, such as low-contrast text and missing alt text, are found on over 50% of the top 1 million website home pages, according to the WebAIM Million study. (12)

"We don't have the budget right now."

If the business owner says they do not currently have the budget for a website evaluation, reinforce that you are selling a website evaluation for just $100. It is a very low-cost way to identify ways to improve customer satisfaction, reduce friction points, and protect against legal risks from non-compliance with accessibility laws.

"We've already worked with a designer."

This response from a business owner indicates that they are aware of the value a designer brings to their business, but that they do not know the difference between a visual designer or a marketing-focused designer and what you can provide. Clarify that your focus is on usability and accessibility, which are often overlooked by designers who focus primarily on aesthetics. This form of a "no" answer can lead to potentially working with the original designer of the website to inform them about accessibility best practices. The kind of collaboration this situation offers is a fantastic opportunity to establish your credibility and expertise with another freelancer or small agency. You may end up with a wonderful working relationship and another reference who can vouch for what you bring to the table.

Thank Them for Their Time

Regardless of the answer you receive, always thank the business owner for their time. Time is the most valuable resource we have as humans, and it is a gift when someone grants you a measure of their time and attention. Demonstrate that you know how valuable it is by being gracious about it. Remember the old adage: "People will forget what you did, but they will always remember how you made them feel." Ensure people feel valued, and they will value you.

WHAT TO DO IF THEY SAY "YES"

While hearing "no" is the most common response, it is also possible that someone will say "yes" to your offer of a website evaluation. Congratulations! It is a fantastic feeling to win a new client. This is a huge step forward in your career, and you should absolutely take a moment to celebrate this win.

When you have had time to relish and celebrate this exciting moment, and you are ready to take the next step, it is time to transition to doing the work. In the next chapter, we will go into detail about how to review a website for accessibility and usability. For now, here are some final takeaways to keep in mind.

Always Get Paid Before Starting the Work

One of the most fundamental principles in freelancing is to never start the work until you have received payment. This ensures that your time and expertise are respected. Setting this professional boundary signals to clients that they should take your services seriously. When considering this part of the transaction, you might think about the benefits of requesting a deposit upfront, followed by gathering the final payment upon completion of the website evaluation. This approach can provide a sense of security for both parties, as it demonstrates commitment from the client, while also assuring you of compensation for your efforts.

Alternatively, opting to take the full payment in advance can be suitable for the size of this project, especially at the rates you are offering.

Ultimately, the payment structure you choose should reflect both the nature of the project and the level of trust you have with the client. By maintaining clear and consistent payment terms, you not only protect yourself and your business interests but also foster a professional and respectful working relationship with your clients.

How You Can Receive Payment

Before starting your outreach, you should set up an easy way for clients to pay you. This might be through mobile applications such as Venmo, Cash App, or Zelle. You could take cash or check and provide a simple receipt via email. Receipts can be created quickly and easily using Google Docs or other word-processing software. An email simply saying, "Your payment of $100 for a Website Accessibility and Usability Evaluation has been received" will also suffice.

If you have a bank account and can set up a Stripe account, you can send very professional-looking invoices and process payments quickly just by having the customer's email. This makes the transaction smooth and simple, yet does not require a lot of effort on your part.

Make sure to explain to the customer that once payment is received, you will begin the evaluation and deliver the report within a set time frame. Within 7–10 business days is a reasonable time frame to complete the website accessibility and usability evaluation. If you finish early, you can surprise and delight your customer with your excellent, prompt service.

Basic Legal Considerations

This book does not constitute legal advice, and it is always recommended that you look for and carefully review relevant laws for your location. That said, it is highly unlikely that you will need to do any legal paperwork to provide a low-cost website evaluation.

If the client appreciates the results of the website evaluation and asks for more extensive work to remediate accessibility issues or implement any of your suggestions, that is up to you to deliver and is not something covered by this book.

For the context of a website evaluation, there are some additional details to be aware of as a freelancer. When offering services to small businesses in the United States, there are a few key legal and tax considerations to be aware of.

Reporting Requirements

If you are offering services as an independent contractor and earn $600 or more from a single client over the course of a year, that client is required to issue you a 1099-NEC form by January 31 of the following year. If you earn less than $600 during the course of the year from one customer, the small business you have provided services for does not need to worry about issuing a 1099-NEC form.

For this service, even though the amount is below the 1099 reporting threshold, you are still required to report the money you received in exchange for your services on your income tax return. You can deduct any business-related expenses incurred to deliver the service (such as travel, software, or materials) from your income, reducing your taxable income.

It may be necessary to explain to the small business that you are an independent contractor and not an employee. This distinction is important for tax purposes, as employees are subject to withholding for Social Security and Medicare, while independent contractors are responsible for handling their own tax payments.

Business Structure

If you're operating as a sole proprietor (freelancer), you can offer services without needing to register a formal business entity, but you'll be responsible for paying self-employment taxes on any income earned. Make sure to track your earnings in a spreadsheet and keep track of any payments received.

If you have a registered business (such as a Limited Liability Company (LLC), S-Corp, etc.), you will need to ensure your business is compliant with any relevant state and local requirements for taxation and reporting. Typically, an LLC can report taxes as part of the individual taxpayer process.

Collecting Sales Tax

Services are generally not subject to sales tax in most states. Some states, however, do tax specific services (such as digital services or certain consulting services). Check the state in which the small business is located to confirm whether your service is taxable.

Written Agreements

These website evaluations can be done informally, at first. It is always a good idea to have a clear written agreement or contract in place for the service you are providing, even for one-off services. This should outline the scope of the service, payment terms, and any other expectations to avoid disputes. For this service, the written agreement can be very simple. A sample basic agreement is provided to readers of this book in the resources area, seen here:

Liability Insurance

Liability insurance is a safety net for unexpected legal claims or client disputes. While it is not legally required for conducting website evaluations, professional liability insurance can be a good investment, especially if you plan to work with larger clients or handle sensitive information. This type of insurance protects you if a client claims that your evaluation or recommendations led to financial loss or legal issues. For example, if the client implements your recommendations and still faces an accessibility-related lawsuit, they could claim your evaluation was inadequate.

Website accessibility is a legal issue (with lawsuits under the ADA and other regulations). If a client follows your advice and later faces legal problems or compliance issues, they might attempt to hold you accountable. This is unlikely when working with small, low-risk clients especially

---

Website Accessibility and Usability Evaluation Service Agreement

This Agreement is made on [Date] between:

Service Provider: [Your Full Name or Business Name], located at [Your Address], hereinafter referred to as the "Consultant."

Client: [Client's Full Name or Business Name], located at [Client's Address], hereinafter referred to as the "Client."

1. Scope of Services

The Consultant agrees to provide a comprehensive **Website Accessibility and Usability Evaluation** of the Client's website located at [Website URL]. The evaluation will assess compliance with **WCAG 2.1 standards** and include recommendations for improving accessibility and usability for users with disabilities. The evaluation will focus on the following areas:

- Keyboard navigation and screen reader compatibility
- Color contrast and text readability
- Mobile and responsive design usability
- Image alt-text and multimedia accessibility
- Any other specific accessibility concerns identified by the Consultant

A written report detailing the findings and actionable recommendations will be provided to the Client.

2. Payment Terms

The total fee for the Website Accessibility and Usability Evaluation is **$[xxx]**.

- Payment is due within **[Number of Days] days** upon receipt of the final report.
- Payment can be made via [Payment Method, e.g., PayPal, Bank Transfer].

FIGURE 3.1 A screenshot of the Website Accessibility and Usability Evaluation Service Agreement provided in the supplemental materials for this book

since your services are limited to providing basic recommendations. If you are only assessing the website without direct implementation or interaction with sensitive data, you may decide that insurance is not necessary.

Limitation of Liability

While liability insurance provides protection in the event of a claim, a well-written service agreement can also limit your liability. Be sure to include clauses about the limitations of your evaluation services, specifying that you do not guarantee full compliance or protection against lawsuits, as well as the extent of your responsibility. To be clear, freelancers and sole proprietors working on small projects or one-time evaluations for low amounts (such as $100) often operate without insurance, though it is still a risk to be aware of.

Example Statement of Limitation of Liability

Here is an example of such a statement (note that this is included in the sample agreement mentioned previously):

"The Consultant will provide the Website Accessibility and Usability Evaluation in good faith and with reasonable care, consistent with industry standards. However, the Consultant makes no guarantees, representations, or warranties, either expressed or implied, regarding the complete accessibility or usability compliance of the website with any specific standards, including but not limited to Web Content Accessibility Guidelines (WCAG) 2.1, ADA, or any other laws or regulations."

"The Client understands and agrees that it is ultimately their responsibility to implement and maintain compliance with accessibility standards and that no audit can ensure 100% compliance due to the dynamic and interpretive nature of accessibility requirements. The Consultant shall not be held liable for any accessibility issues or claims, including legal actions, that arise after the completion of the evaluation."

"In no event shall the Consultant be responsible for any indirect, incidental, special, or consequential damages arising from the results of the evaluation, the Client's implementation of the Consultant's recommendations, or any accessibility issues that are not identified during the evaluation."

Now that you know more about how to sell your services, receive payment, and protect yourself against liability, it is time to do the work. In the next chapter, we will look in depth into each criterion on which to evaluate a website.

CHAPTER 4

*E*VALUATE THE *W*EBSITE

This chapter focuses on the repeatable process of evaluating the usability and accessibility of a website, looking for friction points that turn off potential customers and expose the business to digital accessibility lawsuits.

CONDUCT A STAKEHOLDER INTERVIEW FIRST

The first thing to do when evaluating the business website is to talk to the stakeholders. Ideally, you will set up a phone or video call with the decision-makers for the business. This ensures that everyone involved with the business is confirmed as "on board" with the website evaluation.

Why does this matter? Some business owners can feel protective of what they perceive as "their" property. When you find issues with a website that a business owner has painstakingly built, it's like you're calling their baby ugly. They spent hours and hours learning how to use Wix, WordPress, or Squarespace, and they figured out how to make it look "right" in their own eyes. Their fear is that you, an outsider, are coming in and telling them that they did it wrong. Some folks take this personally, and that's okay. Their business, for better or worse, *is* their baby. Our intention with this website evaluation isn't to tell them that they've done it wrong, but rather to give them the insights they need to refine the website so that they have to perform better and make more money.

In the stakeholder interview, you'll have the opportunity to reassure the business owners of this paradigm and allow them to ask questions.

It is recommended to set up this meeting as a video call, so that you can see their body language and facial expressions. You can "read the room" more effectively when you can see what they're doing when they pause speaking.

Follow a Stakeholder Interview Template

You will want to follow a basic template to guide your questions. The template provided in the supplementary materials (see Figure 4.1) is written in such a way that if coming together for a meeting proves impossible to schedule, you could send the stakeholders the document and have them fill it out individually. The issues you will want to watch out for with this method are timeliness and completeness.

Timeliness

You will want to get started right away, since you have booked this customer for a website evaluation. Unfortunately, sending a document and allowing stakeholders to fill it out in their own time often leads to delays. If they can get it back to you within three days, that is ideal. Past that and the task tends to fall off their list of priorities, and it is difficult to get it back from them without a few back-and-forth emails, which consumes valuable time.

Completeness

Stakeholders often run into problems answering some of the questions when they are filling out the form on their own. They do not understand some of the words, or they are confused about what you mean. Having a call where you ask the questions means you can rephrase questions or use more familiar words for some topics when you see them hesitating to answer. If they do not have you there with them when they are filling out this form on their own, one of two things will happen when they run into a barrier. One, they will give up and set aside the form. This is the main reason why you will not get the form back. Two, they will feel stupid for not knowing something and get too embarrassed to admit that they do not know.

A 30-minute video meeting will allow you to gather all of this information without causing additional stress for the business owners.

[Company Name] Stakeholder Questions

The following are the major questions I usually have as I kick off a redesign. Typically, I would keep this worksheet on my end and fill in the answers as I conduct an interview. Occasionally, it's not possible to meet with the Stakeholder in person, on a video call or even over the phone, so I will share these questions in a document for them to fill. In that instance, I would leave the following lines in the document:

Please feel free to add as many notes or thoughts as you want, I will follow up with any additional questions I have. Add your answers and notes in the table below:

ABOUT CLIENTS/CUSTOMERS

Describe your typical client/customer. (age, life experience, education level, income level, personality traits, etc.)	
How do your clients typically find you?	
What are your clients looking for? How do they think you can help them? *Why do they need [your products or services]?*	
What are a new client's usual questions?	

FIGURE 4.1 A screenshot of the first page of the Stakeholder Questions Form

The stakeholder interview template covers the following topics.

About the Business and Customers

What you are trying to find out is whether the business knows who their Ideal Customer Profile (ICP) is. Who are their target customers and how do those customers find the business? One of my favorite parts of this section is this question: What are a new client's usual questions? This helps you understand what information should be on the website to save the business owner's time. Other questions on this form ask about the business's value proposition and success metrics, and what the business owner wishes people knew before reaching out.

NOTE *An Ideal Customer Profile is a detailed description of a fictional individual or company that represents the perfect customer for your product or service. This profile helps businesses identify and focus their marketing and sales efforts on those who are most likely to benefit from their offerings and, in turn, generate the most value for the business. In UX, we might refer to the ICP as a proto-persona or a user persona, depending on the level of detail.*

Website Design Questions

What value does the website currently deliver to users? What technology is the website running on? What brand styles should the website follow?

My favorite question from this section is the open-ended what do you think your website should be doing for your business that it currently does not? This question gives stakeholders a chance to voice thoughts they think might be irrelevant or "off the wall" but can lead to some details you might not have heard otherwise.

Conducting a stakeholder interview by following this template will ensure you efficiently gather the relevant details for your website evaluation work.

Alternatively, Treat This Like Speculative Work

Alternatively, you could perform the website review speculatively and not involve the stakeholders until after you have conducted the website evaluation. This is a good route to go down if the business is one you are familiar with but the owners or stakeholders have a reputation for being unwilling to take unsubstantiated advice. You can bring the website evaluation results to an initial call and have a solid basis for pitching your redesign services. The "your mileage may vary" adage is apt here. We do not recommend doing work for free, but this method has proven successful for several practitioners.

IDENTIFY THE USER GOALS

Once you have completed the stakeholder interview, you should have a good idea of what the business wants users to do on the website. From there, you will want to identify the main user goals for the website. What are users trying to accomplish on the website?

You might have been taught that you need to conduct user interviews to determine this information, but there is an easier way: visit the website as if you are a user. While there are millions of reasons a website might exist, there are only a handful of actions a user can take to engage with a small business.

If you were a customer of this website, where would *you* start? What would *you* need to do if you wanted to buy something from, book an appointment with, or give something to the organization? This does not need to be a complicated process. Jot down a few notes about what you think a user might want to do on this website and keep them with your stakeholder interview answers.

CONDUCT A WEBSITE EVALUATION

Now that you have some context for the website, review it alongside your Website Accessibility and Usability Evaluation spreadsheet. This is a 125-point checklist for evaluating the usability and accessibility of a website. The spreadsheet has 13 tabs in three major sections:

- First Impressions & 7 Basic Requirements All Websites Need (1 tab)
- Accessibility (1 tab)
- Usability Heuristics (10 tabs)
- Summary (1 tab)

We will discuss the Summary tab in the next chapter. For now, we will review the first three sections and how to use the spreadsheet to evaluate the website.

First Impressions and Seven Basic Requirements

The first tab of the spreadsheet, called Basic Information, is where you will document your first impressions and check for the seven basics that all websites should have. For the First Impressions review checklist (Figure 4.2), you are answering a few simple questions, from your perspective as a person using the internet, not as an expert in whatever topic the website is about. Each of these questions should be answered with Yes or No in the RESPONSE dropdown, and you can leave any additional notes in the Comments / Notes space.

1. Is it clear what purpose the website serves?
2. Is the visual design of the website aesthetically pleasing?
3. Does the website have a cohesive color scheme that is used across all pages of the site?
4. Do you feel like you have enough information to know what to do?
5. Do you feel overwhelmed by information and choices?

First Impressions

Before we dive into the specifics of usability and accessibility, assess your first impression of the website by considering the following prompts.

REVIEW CHECKLIST	RESPONSE
Is it clear what purpose the website serves?	▾
Is the visual design of the website aesthetically pleasing?	▾
Does the website have a cohesive color scheme that is used across all pages of the site?	▾
Do you feel like you have enough information to know what to do?	▾
Do you feel overwhelmed by information and choices?	▾

WEBSITE BASICS	
Website has a Privacy Policy	▾
Website has Terms and Conditions	▾
Website has an Accessibility Statement	▾
Website has a Cookie Policy and Consent Notification	▾
Website has a Data Storage Disclosure	▾
Website has a Copyright Notification	▾
Website is using HTTPS (essential if ecommerce)	▾

FIGURE 4.2 A screenshot of the first tab of the Website Accessibility and Usability Evaluation spreadsheet

Below the REVIEW CHECKLIST section, you'll find a brief list of website basics. These are the elements that should be found on any small business website to meet legal requirements and protect the owners of the website. Before we dig into the comprehensive usability and accessibility evaluation, we will check the website for these basic requirements:

- Privacy policy
- Terms and conditions
- Accessibility statement
- Cookie policy and consent notification
- Data storage disclosure
- Copyright notification
- HTTPS

The check for each basic website element can be answered with Yes or No in the RESPONSE dropdown and, like the previous review checklist items, you can leave notes in the comments section. These notes might include something such as The Privacy Policy was last updated in 2018. It should be reviewed for validity and updated.

Privacy Policy

A privacy policy is essential for a website because it outlines how user data is collected, used, stored, and protected, promoting transparency and enabling users to make informed decisions about sharing their data. It is legally required in many jurisdictions, such as under the General Data Protection Regulation (GDPR) in the European Union and the California Consumer Privacy Act (CCPA) in the United States, to avoid legal consequences and penalties. A clear privacy policy enhances the website's credibility and trustworthiness by showing a commitment to data privacy. It also meets user expectations and contributes to a positive user experience. Additionally, it protects website owners by setting clear guidelines for data handling, reducing the risk of legal disputes, and is often a requirement for partnerships with ad networks, affiliate programs, or business partners.

Terms and Conditions

A terms and conditions page is necessary for a website as it establishes an agreement between the website and its users, outlining what users can and cannot do, which helps ensure fair use and clear expectations. This page provides legal protection for the website owner by resolving disputes and preventing legal issues, clarifying ownership and permissible use of content to prevent misuse, and limiting liability for errors. It also defines user responsibilities, such as safeguarding passwords and not causing harm, and specifies which country's laws govern the websites operations, which is essential for sites with international users. By using the website, users agree to these terms, ensuring they understand their rights and duties, making the website safer and clearer for everyone.

Accessibility Statement

An accessibility statement is important for a website as it outlines the steps taken to ensure accessibility for all users, including those with disabilities, demonstrating compliance with laws such as ADA and WCAG. It builds trust by showing a commitment to inclusivity, improving the business's reputation and potentially expanding its customer base. The statement provides valuable guidance on navigating the website and utilizing accessibility features, and includes a feedback mechanism for reporting issues, allowing proactive improvements and reducing the risk of legal challenges. It serves as a legal defense by documenting ongoing efforts and transparency in addressing accessibility, ultimately protecting the business and enhancing user experience.

Cookie Policy and Consent Notification

A cookie policy and consent notification are necessary for websites to comply with legal requirements, such as the GDPR in the European Union, which mandates informing users about cookie usage and obtaining their consent before using cookies to track website visitor data. These policies respect user privacy by detailing the types of cookies used, the data collected, and how it is used, allowing users to make informed decisions. Transparency about cookie usage builds trust with users, showing that the website values their privacy. Additionally, cookies enhance the user experience by remembering preferences and providing tailored content, but consent is necessary to ensure users are comfortable with this. Proper cookie management helps avoid legal issues and fosters a positive relationship with users.

Data Storage Policy

A data storage policy is required for a website that collects user data as it sets rules for safely managing information gathered from visitors, ensuring responsible data handling and legal compliance. This policy helps the website determine what information to retain, how long to keep it, and how to protect it. By specifying which data is important, setting retention periods, and implementing security measures, the policy safeguards both the website and its users' privacy. It ensures responsible data collection and storage practices, protects user information, and helps the business adhere to privacy laws, thereby preventing legal issues and fostering trust with visitors.

Copyright Notice

A copyright notice is a requirement for any website as it asserts ownership over original content, informing visitors that the content is protected by copyright and that the website or its creators hold the rights to copy, share, display, and modify it. This notice serves as a deterrent against unauthorized use and provides a legal basis for action if infringement occurs. While copyright protection is automatically granted upon the creation of original work, displaying a notice can offer additional legal benefits and serve as evidence in disputes. For websites with an international audience, the notice helps enforce copyright claims worldwide under the Berne Convention. Additionally, it signals the website's commitment to protecting its intellectual property and can be crucial for maintaining certain legal rights, such as seeking damages and attorney fees in a lawsuit.

If the Website Sells Products or Services, Is It Using HTTPS?

HTTPS is essential for websites selling products or services because it ensures data security by encrypting the information exchanged between users and the website, protecting sensitive details such as credit card information and personal data from malicious actors. It provides protection against data theft and cybercrime, reducing the risk of identity theft and fraud. The presence of HTTPS, indicated by a padlock icon or Secure label in the browser, builds trust and credibility among customers, reassuring them that their information is safe. Additionally, e-commerce websites must use HTTPS to comply with PCI DSS requirements. Even non-e-commerce websites benefit from HTTPS through enhanced data privacy, improved search engine optimization (SEO) rankings, increased user trust, and compatibility with modern web features and APIs.

Why HTTPS Matters for Every Website

In the past, HTTPS (HyperText Transfer Protocol Secure) was mainly associated with e-commerce sites handling credit card information. Today, HTTPS is essential for **every** website, regardless of whether you sell products or not. Without it, major browsers like Chrome, Firefox, and Edge may block your site or display a "Not Secure" warning, scaring away visitors before they even reach your homepage.

Think of HTTPS as the difference between sending a sealed letter and writing your private information on a postcard. When you use HTTPS, everything transmitted between your website and the visitor (such as form submissions, login details, or even simple browsing activity) is encrypted, preventing hackers from intercepting and altering data.

Beyond security, HTTPS also improves SEO rankings—Google prioritizes secure websites in search results. Plus, modern features like Progressive Web Apps (PWAs) and certain JavaScript APIs only work on HTTPS-enabled sites.

How SSL Certificates Work

To enable HTTPS, a website needs an SSL (Secure Sockets Layer) certificate, which is like a digital passport for proving your site's identity. When a visitor loads your website, their browser checks your SSL certificate to confirm it's valid and issued by a trusted authority. If the certificate is missing, expired, or incorrectly configured, users may see security warnings.

There are different types of SSL certificates:

- DV (Domain Validation): The most basic and commonly used SSL, verifying that you own the domain.
- OV (Organization Validation): Adds more business verification, showing your organization's name in the certificate details.
- EV (Extended Validation): The highest level of verification, often used by banks and large corporations (used to display a green address bar in older browsers).

How to Check if a Website Has SSL

Not sure if a site has an SSL certificate? Here's how to check:

1. Look at the address bar: Secure websites display a padlock icon next to their URL.
2. Click the padlock: This shows details about the SSL certificate, including who issued it and whether it's still valid.
3. Check the URL: A secure website starts with https:// instead of http://.
4. Use online tools: Websites like SSL Labs' SSL Test (ssllabs.com) let you analyze a site's SSL setup in detail.

How to Get an SSL Certificate for Your Website

If a website doesn't have HTTPS yet, here's how to secure it:

1. Check with your hosting provider – Most web hosts offer free SSL certificates through Let's Encrypt or include SSL in their hosting packages.
2. Use a Content Delivery Network (CDN) – Services like Cloudflare offer free SSL and improve site performance.
3. Purchase an SSL certificate – If you need a higher level of security (e.g., for financial services), you can buy one from a Certificate Authority like DigiCert, GlobalSign, or Sectigo.

4. Install the SSL certificate – Your hosting provider will have a setup guide. For WordPress sites, plugins like Really Simple SSL make it easy.

5. Update your website links – Change any remaining http:// links to https:// to avoid mixed content warnings.

6. Consider a Website Builder – Platforms like Squarespace, Shopify, Wix, and Webflow automatically include SSL certificates for all hosted websites. These platforms handle SSL installation and renewal for you, making them an easy, hassle-free choice for small business owners who don't want to deal with technical configurations. If you use one of these platforms, HTTPS is enabled by default, ensuring your site remains secure with minimal effort.

Troubleshooting Common SSL Issues

Even with HTTPS enabled, some websites encounter problems. Here's how to fix the most common SSL errors:

- "Your Connection is Not Private" Error → Check if your SSL certificate has expired or isn't installed correctly.
- Mixed Content Warnings → Some page elements (like images or scripts) are still loading over HTTP. Use a tool like WhyNoPadlock.com to find and fix them.
- Redirect Loops → If your site keeps redirecting between HTTP and HTTPS, check redirect settings in your hosting panel.

Final Thoughts

Enabling HTTPS isn't just a technical checkbox—it's a must-have for security, trust, and visibility. With a free SSL certificate from Let's Encrypt or a simple setup via your hosting provider, there's no excuse not to protect your site and your visitors. If a business website you're evaluating lacks HTTPS, this should be a top-priority fix!

Once we've evaluated a website for these basics—and documented our findings in the spreadsheet—we can move on to the Accessibility and Usability Heuristics tabs of the spreadsheet. First, however, let us establish some context for how we assess a website.

UNDERSTANDING POUR PRINCIPLES

Before we review a website for accessibility and usability, we first need to understand the principles behind WCAG. The Web Content Accessibility Guidelines are organized by four main principles, which state that website content must be "Perceivable, Operable, Understandable, and Robust." These principles are often referred to by the acronym "POUR," or as the POUR principles.

It is interesting to note that these principles apply to any kind of digital service or product, regardless of the underlying technology. These principles help ensure that everyone, regardless of their abilities, can use and benefit from a website. Here's an easy way to understand them.

Perceivable

Information and UI components must be presented in ways that users can perceive. Everyone should be able to understand the information on your website. It's important to present to users information that can be perceived in different ways. For example, a sighted user might be comfortable watching a video on a website, but a user with vision loss might access that same content using a screen reader to read out the transcript of the video.

Operable

UI components and navigation must be operable. All users, regardless of their level of ability, should be able to interact with and use your website, and it must be functional in ways they can operate. For example, a user with motor disabilities must be able to complete a form using a keyboard and not just using a mouse.

Understandable

Information on the website and the operation of the UI must be understandable to everyone. Instructions and information should be clear and navigation methods should be easy to understand. For example, if the instructions on a website are in a foreign language or full of technical jargon, elderly users or users with cognitive disabilities could get confused and not be able to complete their tasks.

Robust

Website content must be robust enough to be interpreted reliably by a wide variety of users, including those accessing the website with the help of assistive technologies. As technologies evolve, the code and content of the website should remain accessible to all users, including those with common and current assistive devices and tools.

SCORING AND PRIORITIZING

Before moving to the next tab to review the accessibility checklist items, there's an important shift in the information tracked on this and the following 10 tabs: we will add a score for each checklist item.

Scoring

For each item in the checklist, we will assess each page of the website and, after that, assign a score that aligns with how well the website as a whole adheres to the checklist item. The options are Always, Usually, Sometimes, Rarely, Never, and N/A for not applicable.

NOTE *It is rare to mark a checklist item as Always or Never when reviewing a website manually, unless the reviewer is also using supplementary accessibility tools to verify and is checking every page on the website. For that reason, it's best to avoid using these absolutes unless the reviewer is absolutely sure.*

Example: The first checklist item on the Accessibility tab, under Interaction Methods and Modalities, is Interactions do not require a user to use a mouse.

To assess the website for this, the reviewer would visit each page of the website and use their keyboard to navigate through the elements on the page. This is to ensure every interactive element can be reached and activated using the keyboard alone. Dropdowns, modals, and custom widgets should be able to be operated with the arrow keys, Enter, and spacebar. These are not the only interactive elements on a page, so reviewers should be looking for things such as in-line links that are skipped, and other interactive elements that are not triggered by using the keyboard to tab through the page.

If the reviewer is reasonably sure that they have visited all pages of the website and checked that all interactions can be triggered using the keyboard, they can mark that checklist item as Usually and move on to the next checklist item.

If the reviewer finds an interactive element that cannot be triggered by using the keyboard, that element should be noted in the comments section on that row of the spreadsheet. An example is Could not tab to the link in the middle of paragraph 2 under subheading Ways to Connect With Us on the About Us page. If just one or a small number of interactive elements cannot be triggered using the keyboard, all of those instances should be logged as comments. The reviewer might then mark the score as Sometimes or Rarely depending on the context of interactive elements on the site.

This can feel subjective, and that's okay. Some websites will have just a few interactive elements, such as the navigation, in-line links, and a newsletter widget with one form field and one button. Some websites will have many interactive elements, such as media controls, multiple long forms, tabs for on-page navigation within content sections, and many links within the content.

The score will be, by the end of the review, of reasonable accuracy. It primarily allows the reviewer to find critical fixes to prioritize after the review is complete. Don't worry about getting it "right" the first time.

Priority

Reviewers only sometimes use the Priority column and it can also be a subjective rating. Primarily, a priority rating is assigned when an accessibility barrier is found that is both obvious and egregious. Typically, priority is assigned to really impactful issues that impede the use of the website.

Completeness of Assessment

It is important to keep in mind that using this website evaluation spreadsheet will not catch absolutely every accessibility issue that a team of expert accessibility specialists could. Using this process to review a website also costs significantly less than hiring an expert. This review will catch most major accessibility barriers to users. A business owner or a digital technology professional can use the results of this evaluation to determine where to focus redesign and compliance reconciliation efforts first, or whether it is necessary to bring in outside accessibility support.

ACCESSIBILITY TAB

This tab of the spreadsheet is intended to objectively score how easy the website is to use for people of all ability levels and disabilities of all kinds.

We will start with interaction methods and modalities.

Interactions Do Not Require a User to Use a Mouse. Every Functionality Is Fully Keyboard Accessible

This checklist item primarily falls under WCAG Principle 2: Operable. Many individuals cannot interact with a website using a mouse, including those with motor disabilities and visual impairments. Temporary impairments can also make using a mouse difficult. We can check the website for keyboard navigability by loading the website and attempting to navigate through the interface using only the Tab key on our keyboard. We're looking for the following:

- All interactive elements and functions can be reached and activated by using the keyboard alone. This includes opening and closing modals, activating drop-down menus, selecting menu items, closing alerts, submitting forms, and interacting with custom widgets.
- The order of elements focused when navigating using the keyboard is logical and follows the visual layout of the page, moving from top to bottom and left to right.

Target Areas and Calls to Action (CTAs) Are Set to Be at Least 44x44 Pixels

Controls and other interactive elements on a website should be easy to operate. Smaller targets are more difficult to tap or click accurately, especially for users with limited dexterity or hand tremors, or users with visual impairments. Elderly users frequently have trouble selecting small targets. To assess a website for this guideline, we can manually check all interactive elements on a website and measure their size in CSS pixels using developer tools in the browser. We are visually assessing the website for:

- Large buttons that are easy to click
- Clickable icons in a toolbar are distinct and large enough to be tapped or clicked without precision
- Navigation links being adequately spaced and large enough to facilitate easy selection
- Interactive list items, such as lists inside of a drop-down form element, having a height that makes each item easy to select
- Controls providing ample space for selection without the risk of selecting the wrong control (this is especially important for touch targets on mobile devices)

Next, we will look at navigation and wayfinding.

There Are Clear, Visible Indicators Set on All Active Elements as They Receive Focus

Individuals who rely on keyboard navigation require the ability to track their progress through a website. This checklist item is aligned with the POUR principle of Operable and helps users know which element on the screen has keyboard focus. What we're looking for is:

- All interactive elements display a visible focus indicator when navigated to via the keyboard. This could be a border added around an element with CSS, or a vertical bar displaying in a form field indicating the user can insert text.

Pages Have Meaningful Title Text, with Page-Specific Information Going First

Web pages should have titles that describe the topic or purpose. This guideline is essential for improving the accessibility and usability of a website for all users, but especially for users with cognitive disabilities and visual impairments. Consider this example: if an online e-commerce website has product pages with vague titles such as Product 12, a customer may struggle to understand which page they are on. This product page should start with a unique title that indicates the product name and category, such as Men's Casual Shirts – Blue Denim Shirt. This would help the customer quickly identify their location on the website and navigate more efficiently. This enhances the user experience for all customers and can improve sales. The following are what to look for:

- On each page of the website, evaluate the page title and consider whether it is meaningful to the content of the page
- Look at the HTML structure of the page to ensure the <title> tag is used correctly and contains relevant, specific information

Page Titles and Primary Headings (<h1>'s) Are the Same or Similar

This guideline is intended to provide a clear and predictable web page structure for all users, and particularly benefits people by reducing the cognitive load, or mental effort, required to interact with a website. Most users will find a website easier to navigate and comprehend when the biggest, most important heading on a web page has the same or similar text as the page title. Navigate to each page of the website and compare the page `<title>` with the primary heading, or `<h1>`. We're looking for the following:

- The page title tag and `<h1>` tag are aligned in purpose and content
- The text doesn't need to be exactly the same (though it can be), but it should communicate very similar information

Pages Have Meaningful Headings for Each Section

A website should be easy to understand and navigate for all users, and using appropriate headings to create smaller sections of content is an ideal way to ensure that. Users who rely on screen readers benefit from well-defined headings as they can navigate through long pages of complex content using heading shortcuts. For users with cognitive disabilities, clear headings help clarify the structure of the content and make it easier to find relevant information without becoming overwhelmed. To verify adherence, we look for:

- Hierarchical structure (`<h1>`, `<h2>`, `<h3>`, etc.) using descriptive headings
- Smaller "chunks" of content to organize information logically and associate related content effectively

Links' Purpose May Be Discerned from Link Text Alone, or the Immediate Context

By making sure that all links on a website have a clear and discernable purpose, the site becomes more navigable and user-friendly, particularly for those relying on assistive technologies. This enhances the overall accessibility of the website and ensures compliance with WCAG guidelines. Users should be able to understand where a link will take them, reducing confusion and cognitive load. Knowing the purpose of a link beforehand also helps users with motor disabilities determine whether it's worth the effort to navigate to a link. What we're looking for in our website review:

- Link text that is clearly worded and specific. For example:
  - A link that says **Click here to donate now for disaster relief** is more effective than just **Click here**
  - A link that says **Learn more about our mission** instead of **More** makes the link's purpose clear

A "Skip Link" Is Provided at the Very Top of the Page and Is Revealed on Focus

People with visual impairments may use a screen reader to navigate through a website and this link allows these users to bypass repetitive navigation links and directly jump to the main content of the page. This skip link is also helpful for individuals with motor disabilities, as it reduces the number of keystrokes needed to navigate through the site. Having a skip link at the top of the page is especially necessary for websites with a dense, multi-level navigation menu. We can test this guideline on any website by waiting for the page to load completely and then pressing the Tab key once. Here's what we are looking for:

- A previously invisible button or link should become visible at the top of the page, before other content, when it receives focus
- The button or link should say something such as: **Skip to main content**
- Clicking on the link or button should bypass all navigational elements on the page and display the main content section of the web page
- The skip link should have high contrast between the text and the background color and be distinct from all other elements
- The skip link should be consistently placed at the top of all pages, maintaining uniformity across the site

Organization of Navigation Is Logical and Facilitates Users Finding What They Need

Menu items should be labeled logically according to the content of the page. Smaller websites with a limited number of pages will pass this check easily. A small number of menu items makes the interface easy to process, even for users unfamiliar with the website.

An e-commerce website with a large number of items, however, would benefit from implementing effective navigation that reduces the need for extensive browsing. Features to implement could include categorizing products into clearly defined sections and providing multiple ways to access these categories, such as through a top menu, search bar, and filters. Implementing breadcrumb trails and clear labels would further enhance navigability, making it much easier for all users to find products quickly and efficiently.

When reviewing a website for logical navigation and wayfinding, we are looking for:

- Consistent navigation across all pages of the website, helping users learn and remember navigation pathways
- Breadcrumb trails that provide a clear path from the home page to the current page, allowing users to track their navigation history and content
- Clear menu labels using easy-to-understand language
- Accessible website search to help users quickly find pages or items, reducing the need to navigate through multiple layers
- Filtering options on shopping sites to help narrow down categories or preferences, making it easier for users to find specific items

Next, we will review structure and semantics.

Content That Looks like a Heading Is Defined as Such

The relevant guidelines require that the visually implied relationship between pieces of information on a web page be supported programmatically. If content that looks like a section title (because it was assigned larger text, bolded font, etc.) is not marked as a heading using appropriate HTML tags, users with visual impairments or cognitive disabilities will not be aware of the importance or structure of the information, or understand the relationship between a title and body content. To assess a website for this criterion:

- Review the HTML to ensure that elements appearing as headings use the correct heading tags (`<h1>`, `<h2>`, etc.)
- Consider navigating the website with a screen reader to check whether it reads the headings in a way that reflects the visual hierarchy

Heading Structure Hierarchy Does Not Skip Any Levels

Along with headings that look like headings and are marked up in HTML appropriately, it's important to verify that website content does not skip any levels. Users relying on screen readers navigate through content by jumping from one heading to another. Skipping heading levels can cause confusion and misinterpretation of the heading structure. A logical order of headings and content allows users to efficiently move through content without unnecessary confusion or back-tracking. For users with situational disabilities or temporary impairments, such as those working in distracting environments, well-structured headings help quickly locate and comprehend sections of interest. Reviewing a website for heading structure hierarchy includes:

- Inspecting the HTML to verify that heading tags (<h1>, <h2>, <h3>, etc.) are used sequentially without skipping levels

Navigation Menus Are Structured Using Lists

Websites should use lists for navigation. This is the best practice because, by default, screen readers "know" what lists are and how to navigate them. Many websites use HTML elements such as <div> and <span> to create navigation menus. These elements can be improved using specific code properties with Accessible Rich Internet Application code (often referred to as simply ARIA) to provide additional information to screen readers. This works, but it's a complex way of "fixing" a poor design. Lists that are formatted correctly are accessible by default. To review a website for this:

- Inspect the website navigation menu and verify that the HTML tags being used for menu items are <li> (list item) elements contained within a <ul> (unordered list) element
- The menu <ul> and nested items <li> might be nested within a <nav> container, which is an even more specific HTML tag that communicates to the browser and screen reader about that UI element

Form Controls (Inputs) Are Assigned a Meaningful, Visible Text Label

Visible, meaningful text labels for form controls are necessary for users with visual impairments, cognitive disabilities, and motor disabilities. Labels ensure that these users can understand and interact with the form fields correctly. If form controls lack meaningful labels, any user might miss important information, leading to errors or incomplete submissions. When reviewing a website, this might include:

- Visually checking that all form fields have labels that are visible on the screen, and are not just placeholder text that disappears when the user starts typing
- Inspecting the HTML to ensure that label tags are properly used and associated with form controls using the for attribute linking to the ID of the input field
- Using automated tools can identify any forms missing proper label associations

Groupings of Form Elements Share a Common Group Label

Grouping related form elements with a common label helps users with cognitive disabilities and visual impairments understand the relationship between fields, making them easier to navigate and complete. With this guideline, we are checking that input elements that are associated together share a common label. An example of this is a form where the First Name and Last Name input fields are separated but share a common Name label. Similarly, a checkout form taking in a shipping address from a customer might include Street Address, City, Zip Code, and Country as separate fields, but they are all part of the user's address. To identify whether a web page has done this:

- Check that related form fields are grouped together and have a common label that clearly identifies their relationship
- Use the browser developer tools to inspect the HTML and visually verify

Information Conveyed Through Sensory Characteristics Is Also Supported in Text

This guideline is essential because it ensures that information is accessible to all users, regardless of their sensory perception abilities. Users who are blind or have low vision may not be able to perceive visual cues such as color, shape, or location, which are often used to communicate information. Similarly, users with hearing impairments may miss information conveyed solely through auditory means, such as sound alerts, without a text alternative. Users experiencing temporary impairments such as busy or noisy environments will benefit from information being communicated in more than one medium, too. When reviewing a website for adherence to this guideline, we want to do the following:

- Check the website manually to identify any instances where information is conveyed using sensory characteristics (such as color, shape, sound, or location) without text support
- Use automated testing tools to identify any potential sensory characteristic issues. These tools will highlight elements that may rely solely on color or other sensory means

Data Tables Are Clearly Assigned Header Columns and/or Rows

Data tables often overwhelm users with information, no matter their level of ability or disability. Ensuring that data tables are assigned meaningful heading information for columns and rows reduces cognitive load for all users, but in particular benefits users with visual impairments and cognitive disabilities by helping these users understand the relationship between the data in the context of its headers. When reviewing a website, we are looking for specific HTML elements to be used for data tables:

- Review the data table to verify that the heading of the column or row is visually distinct from the content in the table cells
- Inspect the HTML to verify that table headers are marked up with specific table header `<th>` tags, not just visually distinguished with bold text, and are associated with their respective table data `<td>` elements
- Ensure that all tables on the website use the proper HTML elements, such as table header `<thead>`, table body `<tbody>`, and table foot `<tfoot>` sections, to appropriately and logically structure the data

The next section to review is error prevention and states.

Labels and Instructions Are Worded in Text to Provide Users with Adequate Support

Users who rely on assistive technology to understand a website will find labels and instructions that are provided in an image inaccessible, leading to errors and incomplete submissions. All users benefit from clearly worded instructions provided in textual format. Review a website as follows:

- Ensure all form fields have clear, text-based labels and instructions
- Use automated accessibility testing tools that can identify forms lacking proper text labels and instructions

Labels and Instructions Are Located in Close Proximity to Their Controls

Users with low vision or cognitive disabilities benefit from having labels located near form inputs, making it easier to associate text with corresponding fields. People using screen magnifiers can lose context for the information they are asked to input if form labels are located too far from the input. Do the following:

- Check that labels are adjacent to their respective form fields, either to the left or directly above them

Required Fields Are Identified as Such in the Label Text

Identifying required fields in a form using label text, rather than just a red asterisk, is essential for several reasons, particularly in terms of accessibility and usability. Using text labels for required fields maintains consistency and clarity across all forms, ensuring that users always understand which fields are mandatory.

Screen readers, which are primarily—but not exclusively—used by visually impaired users, read out text labels but may not always recognize or convey the meaning of visual symbols such as a red asterisk. A visually impaired user navigating a form with a screen reader might miss the asterisk, leading to confusion about which fields are mandatory.

Users with cognitive disabilities might find it challenging to understand symbols or might miss the significance of a red asterisk. They might see it but misunderstand its importance. Users with color blindness may not distinguish the red asterisk from the rest of the text or background, making it difficult for them to identify required fields.

A compliant form will have labels such as Password (required) and Confirm Password (required) to meet regulatory standards. When reviewing a website:

- Look at all form fields. Form fields that are required should have a text label that says **required** in clearly visible text.
- Document any instances where just an asterisk is used to indicate required, no matter what color it is.

Users Are Not Required to Remember Information Between Pages in a Multi-Step Process

This guideline directly supports users with cognitive, memory, or learning disabilities by reducing their cognitive load and reliance on memory for tasks. Many users find it challenging to recall information previously entered, regardless of their disability, including users who are temporarily impaired by stress or anxiety, or who are in a distracting environment. Evaluate a website for compliance with this guideline:

- Review each form-filling process to identify any points where users must remember information from one part of the process to another
- Check for a review page summarizing all entered information, providing users with an opportunity to confirm or edit details without needing to navigate back through the process

- Document any opportunities to automatically populate previous data provided by the user

The next section to review is contrast and legibility.

Body Text (and Other Small Text) Should Have a Contrast Ratio of at Least 4.5:1

Any normal text that is not a heading must have a contrast ratio between the text color and the color of the background behind the text of at least 4.5:1. To review a website for compliance with this guideline:

- Use a contrast-checking tool, such as the industry-recognized WebAIM Contrast Checker (*https://webaim.org/resources/contrastchecker/*) to check for this ratio
- These colors can also be found by taking a screenshot and using a color selector tool to capture the hex codes of the text and background colors

Large Text Should Have a Contrast Ratio of at Least 3:1

Large text such as headings must have a contrast ratio between the text color and the color of the background behind the text of at least 3:1. Evaluators can use the same contrast-checking tool as used for body text contrast. The WebAIM Contrast Checker tool also provides visual guidance about the pass/fail status of the contrasting colors for normal text, large text, and graphical objects such as form elements and other UI components.

Link Text Copy Has a Contrast Ratio of at Least 3:1 Against Its Surrounding Text

When inline links are used, the contrast ratio of the link text color and the background color should be at least 3:1. To review a website for this contrast, use the same contrast checker as with body text and large text. The link text color should also maintain a contrast ratio against the background color that aligns with the size of the text, as covered in the previous two criteria.

Foreground/Background Contrast Ratio of Meaningful Graphics Is at Least 3:1

In the context of WCAG, a "meaningful graphic" refers to any visual element that conveys essential information for understanding the content or interacting with the website. This includes icons, buttons, charts, infographics, and other graphical UI elements integral to the user's experience. Ensuring that these graphics are easily visible to users with visual impairments, such as those with color vision deficiencies, requires a contrast ratio of 3:1. This means the brightness of the foreground (the graphic itself) should be three times the brightness of the background, making it stand out clearly. To review meaningful graphics on a website:

- Find the colors of the image using any online tool. Search for an image color picker and upload the image, then select colors from around the edges of the image to check the contrast against the background color of the page. Some images have a lot of variation around the edge of the photo or graphic, and others have just one background color. Check all colors to ensure sufficient contrast between the image and the web page

- Use the same color-contrast-checking tool as with text content

NOTE *The contrast of some images might make it difficult to capture all colors around the edge. A simple fix for this guideline would be to add a single-color border around an image to distinguish it clearly from the background.*

Images Do Not Have Text Embedded in Them

It is important to avoid embedding text into images for several key reasons, particularly related to accessibility, usability, and SEO. Screen readers, used by visually impaired users, cannot read text that is embedded within images. They can only read actual text on the web page or alt text provided for images. Text embedded in images does not resize or reflow like actual text, leading to readability issues on different screen sizes, particularly on mobile devices. Search engines index actual text on web pages to determine content relevance. Text embedded in images is not indexed, which can negatively impact the website's search engine ranking. Embedding text in images also makes it difficult to update the site frequently and easily, which can prove problematic for websites with many products. Review the website for adherence to this guideline:

- Check whether text is embedded in images. If it is, replace it with actual text on the web page and provide descriptive alt text for the images

- It is okay to have instances where text is embedded in an image, but make sure the exact same information is also presented in the body text

Line Spacing (Also Known as Leading) Is Set to at Least 1.5 in Paragraphs, and Twice as Much Between Paragraphs

This guideline primarily refers to blocks of text. Adequate line spacing improves readability for users with cognitive disabilities and low vision by preventing text from appearing cluttered and enhancing overall text clarity. A website with tightly packed text and very little spacing between paragraphs can make it difficult for users to process information. Assess a website for this guideline:

- Inspect the CSS to ensure line spacing in paragraphs is set to at least 1.5 times the font size, and spacing between paragraphs is twice the font size

Selected Typefaces Are Easy to Read and Render Properly on Mobile

Properly rendering typefaces, or fonts, ensures readability for users of all types, including those with impaired vision or cognitive disabilities. Providing a consistent and clear text presentation is essential for a good user experience. Fonts without decorative elements (serifs) are generally easier to read on screens. Examples include Arial, Helvetica, and Verdana.

- Check that body typefaces render properly on multiple mobile devices, as well as different screen sizes and resolutions
- Check that the font has characters that are distinct and easily distinguishable from others Look for characters such as "I" (uppercase i), "l" (lowercase L), and "1" (one) to see whether they look similar
- Confirm that display font types are not being used for body text. If these fonts are part of the website's branding, ensure they are only used for large-size text and brief segments of text

The next section to review is language and readability.

Content Is Designed in Short Blocks of Text That Are Easier to Manage Cognitively

Many users struggle with large blocks of text on websites, finding it hard to read and comprehend the content. Users with visual impairments, cognitive disabilities, and attention disorders can benefit from making content more manageable and less overwhelming. Long articles with no subheadings, or pages with long, dense paragraphs, are difficult to process. Review the website:

- Identify long blocks of text on websites and document where they are found. Update the content and break large passages into smaller "chunks" of information where possible

- Check for multiple levels of heading hierarchy and document passages where subheadings might be appropriate to add

- Make note of instances where reformatting content into lists might provide more meaning or have a greater impact on users

Headings and Form Labels Are Worded So They Are Meaningful to Users

A user might be confused by vague or unclear headings and button labels, leading to difficulty completing tasks or comprehending instructions. The user experience is greatly enhanced by providing clear and descriptive labels and headings that aid in understanding and navigation. Check the website for:

- Page headings and section headings that clearly describe the immediately following content

- Form labels that clearly communicate the input expected from the user

Changes in Language Within the Page Are Specified for Assistive Technologies

This guideline is specifically referring to the human language of the page. Guideline 3.1.2, Language of Parts, explains that, to pass this heuristic, "the human language of each passage or phrase in the content can be programmatically determined" with some exceptions for proper names, technical terms, and a few other examples. In the code of the page, it should be specified what language the text is in. To check a website:

- In the browser, right-click on the web page and inspect the code. Check the `<html>` tag at the very top of the code to see whether there is a lang attribute specifying the default language of the document. For example, it might say `<html lang="en">` indicating that the language of the page is English.

- For quotes in another language, each quote should be surrounded by a `<span>` tag inserting the correct language attribute. For a quote in French, we might see the following: `<p>`This is in English. `<span lang="fr">`Ceci est en français.`</span></p>`.

Content Is Made Easier to Understand by Leveraging Plain Language Principles

The website should use words, phrases, and concepts familiar to the user, rather than industry-oriented technical terms and jargon. This criterion focuses on ensuring that text on a website is readable and understandable for as many users as possible. This guideline is dependent on the context and audience, but to be sure your website can be understood by the widest audience, writing in language understood by people with a lower secondary education reading level is ideal, unless more complex language is necessary for the content. This is beneficial for aging users, people with cognitive and learning disabilities, non-native speakers, and people experiencing a temporary impairment, such as being under stress or side effects from medication. To evaluate a website for this guideline:

- Evaluate the text on the site using readability tools
- Look for tooltips or links to definitions for complex terms
- Look for opportunities to replace jargon with plain language explanations

Next, review the section on predictability and consistency.

Repeated Elements Are Consistent Throughout the Website

This guideline encourages us to make website pages appear and operate in predictable ways. It's essential that websites provide ways to help users navigate, find content, and determine where they are. To evaluate a website for this guideline:

- Review all pages of the website to ensure navigation elements are consistent in location, style, and function
- Navigation menus should appear at the top of every page without variation in position
- The website should use the same terminology for common functions (for example, it shouldn't say Create in one place and Add in another, if they do the same thing, or, similarly, Submit and Enter)

- Drop-down menus and other interactive elements should have a uniform interaction and work the same on every page
- Navigation links should be in the same predictable order on every page to prevent disorientation

The Number of Steps Required to Complete an Action Are Minimal

While the "three-click rule"—stating that it should always be possible for a user to find the required information in three or fewer clicks—has largely been debunked, it is still essential to provide users with a streamlined, simple process for completing tasks. Fewer steps reduce cognitive load, making processes easier to understand and complete successfully. For users with motor impairments, this guideline is crucial for reducing the physical effort required by users with limited dexterity or motor function. Simplifying processes helps those who use screen readers or magnification technology by making navigation more efficient. To assess a website for adherence to this guideline:

- Break down the steps required for core tasks and identify unnecessary complexities. Where possible, use a single-page process that groups all necessary fields logically
- Look for opportunities to leverage progressive disclosure and only show additional options or fields when relevant to the user's choices. This can help keep initial views and actions simple
- When possible, review performance metrics for complex processes to measure how long it takes users to complete tasks and how many errors they encounter
- Review forms for any fields that are not absolutely necessary, and use smart defaults where possible

Functionalities and Features Are Easily Discoverable

Being able to find core functions on a website is critical to reducing frustration and error rates that potentially deter users from fully engaging with a website. Discoverability reduces the need for extensive or precise movements for users with motor control issues and reduces confusion and cognitive load for all users. Review a website:

- Check for a search bar at the top of every page. A robust search can help users quickly find specific information or features

- Make sure navigation menus are well organized and logically ordered. Clear labels make it easier to discover different sections of the website

- Look for support documentation and informative tours that guide new users through key features when they first visit the site

Both Portrait and Landscape Orientations Are Supported

Users should be able to access and interact with content regardless of the orientation of their device. This is helpful for individuals with physical disabilities who might use devices in fixed orientations due to mounts on wheelchairs or other mobility aids. These users need the flexibility to use websites in their preferred orientation. This guideline also ensures that websites accommodate personal preferences and environmental constraints such as charging a device while using it, which may limit how it can be held. Testing for this guideline involves the following:

- Check the website on various devices, including smartphones and tablets, to ensure that it operates correctly in both landscape and portrait orientations

- Look for responsive menus that adapt, collapsing into a "hamburger" menu in portrait mode but expanding horizontally in landscape

- Check that forms adjust input fields and buttons to be easily accessible in both orientations

- Text and images should resize and reflow to remain readable and navigable without loss of information or functionality

- Look for rotational prompts that, instead of restricting orientation, encourage users to rotate their device if it enhances usability for certain tasks, such as viewing a detailed chart

Users Are Informed When Providing Input Triggers a Change of Context

This criterion specifies that changing the setting of any UI component should not automatically cause a change of context unless the user has been advised to expect that behavior before using the component. Sudden changes can be disorienting or confusing for people with cognitive disabilities and visual impairments. Knowing in advance what to expect helps users prepare for and understand the interaction. For individuals with motor disabilities, if a change of context is triggered without warning, it could lead to errors and difficulty in navigation. Users in unfamiliar environments or under stress benefit from predictable inter-actions to avoid mistakes.

- Navigate through the website and monitor what happens when inputs are provided by the user. Ensure no unexpected changes occur without prior warning.
- Look for icons or text notifications beside links that indicate if the page will open in a new browser window. Test each link to verify the expected action.
- In the code, look for event handlers (such as onChange) that trigger changes of context without user confirmation or notification.
- For settings or selections that change context, look for buttons that confirm changes before activating.

Users Are Informed When Setting the Focus on a Control Triggers a Change of Context

When a UI component receives focus, it should not initiate a change of context for the user without notification. This might look like a drop-down selection that takes the user to a new view in a complex dash-board. Users who rely on screen readers may not realize the page has reloaded, disorienting them. Ideally, a context change should require a user-initiated action—such as selecting a button. Check a website for this guideline by doing the following:

- Navigate the website using keyboard controls to check whether focusing on any element changes the context without warning
- Review the code for onFocus event handlers that might trigger con-text changes and refactor them
- Look for clear instructions before controls that might lead to context changes to ensure users are informed of what to expect

The next section to review is timing and preservation.

Users Are Provided with a Mechanism to Ask for Time Extensions Ahead of Time

This guideline is applicable to any website where the user is given a period of time to complete an action, such as buying tickets for an event or booking a flight. This criterion ensures users are given ade-quate time to interact with content. Many users benefit from websites that accommodate this guideline: people with cognitive disabilities may need more time to read and understand instructions. Elderly users with slower physical and cognitive responses may require more time to complete tasks. Users with temporary impairments, such as an injury or recovering from surgery, could benefit from having more time to interact with content, type, or navigate between interactive elements.

Examples of what this guideline might look like on a website are online exams, shopping cart checkout, complex financial forms, banking session timeouts, and reservation systems. To evaluate how well a website meets this guideline:

- Navigate through the site to identify any timed sessions or processes. Verify whether the site offers options to extend these time limits.

- Use tools to determine whether time adjustments are programmatically possible and whether alerts about time limits are properly announced by accessibility aids.

Upcoming Session Timeouts Are Clearly Identified as Such in the Design

Similar to the previous checklist criterion, this guideline ensures all users, particularly those with disabilities, have sufficient time to complete tasks without stress or error. If session timeouts are not clearly indicated, a user with a motor impairment who takes longer to type may find themselves logged out before completing the form, leading to data loss and a need to start over. Assess a website for this criterion:

- Navigate through the website to determine whether any session timeouts are used and check whether those timeouts are communicated to the user

- Use a screen reader to ensure that any alerts or warnings are readable by screen readers and that they are announced in a timely manner

- Review the website's policies for statements about session timeouts and user options to manage them

Users Can Turn Off, Adjust, or Extend Time Limits When Sessions Are About to Run Out

People with disabilities may need more time to complete actions on a website. This criterion helps ensure that users can complete tasks without experiencing unexpected changes in content or context as a result of a time limit. To check for adherence to this guideline:

- Test timeout adjustability by manually engaging in timed activities on the website to see whether they can be adjusted by the user
- Confirm that the website's policy clearly informs users of their ability to manage time limits

Options to Postpone or Suppress Interruptions Are Offered. Users Should Be Able to Request Content Updates Rather Than Content Being Updated Automatically

This guideline is related to the previous criterion and ensures that all users, especially those with certain disabilities or impairments, can access content without distraction or difficulty. If users need more time to process information, it should be possible to reduce interruptions and distractions. Examples of this guideline in a UI include news tickers, stock tickers, auto-refresh feeds on social media websites or plugins, pop-up notifications, slideshows and carousels, and videos that automatically play once the page is loaded. Assess a website for compliance with this guideline:

- Check that all elements that automatically update or cause interruptions have visible controls to pause, stop, or hide updates or notifications

There Are Mechanisms to Save Data and Allow Data Recovery After User Re-Authenticates

When a user's session expires and logging in again is necessary, no data previously entered by the user is lost due to session expiration. Like with the previous timing-related criterion, this ensures users who require more time to complete tasks have the time they need. Consider a user who is filling out a detailed application form on a government website. The form takes significant time due to the complexity and the detailed information required. If the session times out without saving the data, the user would have to start over, leading to a frustrating user experience, loss of data, and decreased trust in the website. This can potentially deter users from completing essential tasks online. To ensure a website meets this criterion:

- Test how the website handles session timeouts by engaging with a form or application process until the session expires to see whether the data is preserved

- Analyze the re-authentication workflow to ensure that the steps required are straightforward and limited in complexity

Next, we check for movement and flashing

Moving and/or Animated Content Can Be Paused, Stopped, or Hidden

For many people, continuous movement can cause distractions, or even physical reactions such as seizures in people with photosensitive epilepsy. For any elements on the page that move, flash, or are otherwise animated, there should be control mechanisms for the user to pause, stop, or hide them. Animated, moving, or flashing content should not distract or harm the user. Violating this guideline can lead to users not being able to consume content effectively, potentially causing them to leave the website or, worse, suffer discomfort or health issues. Review a website for this criteria:

- Navigating through the website and looking for any moving elements. Ensure that controls to pause or stop them are present and functional

Video and Audio Files Are Not Set to Auto-Play

Unexpected audio can be disorienting or painful, especially for users with hearing aids. Auto-playing media can make it difficult for users with cognitive disabilities to concentrate on other parts of the web page. For users with visual impairments, sudden sounds might mask critical speech output from screen readers, complicating navigation and interaction. Users in a noisy environment, or those in a quiet setting (such as a library or open office), may find automatically playing audio disruptive. Review a website for adherence to this criterion:

- Check that videos do not auto-play without a user explicitly starting it
- Look for visible, functional controls for playing and pausing the content
- Look for settings to remember user preferences for video playback across sessions

Audio Volume Is Adjustable via a Visible, Labeled Control

Loud or uncontrollable audio can distract or even distress some users, making accessing the website difficult. Users who are hard of hearing may need to adjust the volume to better hear audio content without affecting system-level sound settings. Being able to control audio volume helps minimize cognitive overload for users with cognitive disabilities or sensory sensitivities. These users benefit from having the ability to control volume to interact comfortably with a website. Assess a website for the following:

- Audio controls should be visible and in close proximity to every audio and video player on a website
- The audio slider control should be clearly labeled with icons and text
- Check for settings that remember user-set volume levels during the session or across visits through cookies or user profiles

Flashing or Blinking Effects Are Slower Than Three Times per Second

This guideline is crucial for providing a safe environment for users with photosensitive epilepsy and other neurological disorders. These users can experience seizures triggered by flashing lights and certain visual patterns that appear on screens. Violating this guideline can lead to serious health risks for users susceptible to seizures and greatly hinder the accessibility of a website. Individuals with migraine and other visual disorders can have a medical episode triggered by rapid flashing. Users with autism can be sensitive to visual stimulation, which can be disturbing or distracting. Even individuals without a diagnosed condition might experience discomfort or nausea from rapid flashing, especially in dimly lit environments. Ensure a website adheres to this guideline:

- Look for any flashing effect on the website and ensure the effect is limited to less than three times per second. Consider what value this effect brings to the website and whether the potential adverse effects are worth it.
- Check that users have the option to skip any elements with flashing effects or disable them entirely.
- Consider what alternative animations could be used that do not rely on flashing or blinking effects.

Our final accessibility evaluation section is visual and auditory alternatives.

Understanding the different classifications of images as defined by WCAG is essential. These distinctions help ensure that websites are accessible to all users, including those with disabilities. Here's a breakdown of the different types of images and how they should be handled.

Informational Images Are Provided With Meaningful Alt Text Describing Their Content

Informational images convey simple concepts or information that are not represented by text elsewhere on the page. Examples include icons that display visually what they represent (such as a printer icon to indicate the print function), photographs of products, or maps.

Each informational image should have an alt attribute that describes the image's specific function or content concisely. The description should convey the same message that the image does visually.

Example: A photograph of a product for sale on an e-commerce site should have alt text describing what the product is, possibly including color and relevant details.

How to check the website:

- Check that each image has concise yet descriptive alt text that explains what is shown, such as: Purple hibiscus flower Hawaiian shirt short sleeve linen with single breast pocket

Decorative Images Are Identified So They Can Be Ignored By Assistive Technologies

Decorative images are used purely for visual enhancement and do not convey important content or instructions. These might include stylistic borders, flourishes, or images used as part of the page background.

Decorative images should be implemented in a way that can be ignored by assistive technology. This is typically done by setting the alt attribute to alt="" (empty alt attribute), ensuring screen readers skip over them.

Example: A floral border image that serves no functional purpose other than making the website aesthetically pleasing should have an empty alt attribute.

How to check the website:

- Look for decorative images and check that they have empty alt tags (alt="") or are implemented via CSS

Active Images Are Provided With Meaningful Alt Text Describing Their Purpose

Active images are those that act as controls or provide functionality, such as buttons or clickable icons. These images initiate actions or link to other pages. The alt text for active images should describe the action that will occur when interacted with, not just what the image looks like.

Example: An image used as a submit button in a form should have alt text such as Submit form or Search depending on its function, rather than just Button.

How to check the website:

- Look for clear alt text assigned to each image button, such as Add to Cart, Remove Item, or Checkout

Complex Images Are Given Alt Text and An Extended Full Text Description

Complex images contain substantial information—much like charts, graphs, diagrams, or illustrations that cannot be fully described in a brief alt text. These images might include bar charts representing data or diagrams showing workflows.

How to label: Complex images should be accompanied by longer descriptions that explain the content displayed in the image. This might be done through a detailed caption, a descriptive summary beside the image, or a link to a full page with an extended description.

Example: A bar graph showing the annual sales data for a company over five years should have brief alt text, such as "Bar graph of annual sales from 2015 to 2020" and a more detailed description or a link to a detailed description available nearby or on a referenced page.

How to check a website:

- Review complex images and ensure each has an appropriately descriptive alt text and links to detailed descriptions

  IMPORTANT: For all images on a website, navigate the site using a screen reader to ensure it reads the alt text for all images (except decorative images with empty alt text attributes) and can access detailed descriptions.

Transcripts Are Provided for Audio-Only and Video-Only Content

Providing transcripts is required to support users who are deaf or hard of hearing, as they rely on text to understand audio content. It also helps users with cognitive disabilities who may find it easier to understand written content, and non-native speakers who benefit from reading along. Review the website to check:

- Each instance of audio-only or video-only content has an accompanying transcript that is easily accessible

Synchronized Captions Are Provided for Pre-Recorded Videos

Synchronized captions are essential for users who are deaf or hard of hearing, allowing them to follow along with the spoken content and other relevant sounds in videos. Captions also benefit non-native speakers and users in noisy environments. A deaf user watching an instructional video without captions would miss all the spoken information, making the video unusable. Check the website for the following:

- Play pre-recorded videos and check whether they have synchronized captions available. Look for a CC button or similar option to enable captions

Audio Description Tracks Are Provided for Pre-Recorded Videos

Audio descriptions provide support for users who are blind or have low vision, providing them with descriptions of visual content that is important for understanding the video. A blind user trying to watch a video that shows important visual information without audio descriptions would miss critical content. Assess the website for this criterion:

- Check whether pre-recorded videos on the website have audio description tracks. Look for options to enable audio descriptions or check the video settings for this feature

Transcript Content Is Formatted for Scannability and Readability

Well-formatted transcripts help users with cognitive disabilities, deaf or hard-of-hearing users, and those with temporary impairments. Accurate timestamps, speaker identification, and descriptions of non-speech content make the transcripts easier to follow and understand. A user with cognitive disabilities might struggle to follow a poorly formatted transcript with no clear structure, making it difficult to understand the content. A transcript that is just a block of text without timestamps or speaker identification would fail this heuristic. A compliant example would format the transcript with timestamps, clearly marked speakers, and descriptions of relevant non-speech audio content. Check the website as follows:

- Review the transcripts provided for audio and video content. Check for clear formatting, accurate timestamps, identification of each speaker, and inclusion of descriptions for non-speech content such as sound effects

We've completed our initial assessment for website accessibility! Your spreadsheet should have a colorful array of scores and many notes. The next 10 tabs of the evaluation spreadsheet are much shorter and focus primarily on usability. Onward!

TAB 1: WAYFINDING AND ORGANIZATION

Using the criteria on this tab, we will evaluate a website's usability regarding wayfinding and organization of information. What we're doing here is making sure users know where they are and what to do next in their journey.

The User Understands Where They Are Within the Website

This guideline ensures that all users, especially those with disabilities, can orient themselves within a website, navigate through it effectively, and complete tasks efficiently. Clear navigational cues and consistent page structure help reduce confusion and guide the user to desired actions. Navigational aids can support wayfinding for users unfamiliar with the interface, especially when completing complex tasks. To assess a website for this guideline, check that:

- Navigation menu styles are used to indicate what page of the website the user is currently on
- Breadcrumbs are available to navigate within complex categories
- Navigation is visible or easily accessible to the user at all times

Menu and Button Labels Have the Keyword(s) First, Forming Unique Labels with Semantic Meaning

Headings and labels on a website should be clear and descriptive to help all users understand the purpose of content and interactive elements. This supports independent navigation and wayfinding, even for users with disabilities or who are using assistive technology. Using vague button labels such as More or Add might cause some users to misunderstand the importance of the interaction and potentially abandon their task. Descriptive and keyword-first labels such as Add to Cart immediately inform users of the button's function, which facilitates a smoother experience. When reviewing a website for this guideline, do the following:

- Review all menus and button labels on the website, using browser tools to inspect the HTML if necessary
- Ensure that the most important keyword is placed at the beginning of the label. For example, use Add to Cart instead of Click Here to Add
- Verify that each label clearly and uniquely describes its function or destination. Labels should not be ambiguous or repetitive

Related and Interdependent Form Fields Appear on the Same Screen in All Situations

Information, structure, and relationships displayed through consistent and logical grouping help reduce the cognitive load of users, making it easier to process and understand information. When related fields are on the same screen, it's easier for those using screen magnifiers or screen readers to navigate and understand the context without having to switch between different screens or tabs. Keeping related fields together reduces the need for extensive navigation, which can be physically taxing for those with limited dexterity.

This guideline is related to complex forms and processes. For example, a medical clinic has an online form for patients to fill out prior to their first visit. Patients need to enter their extensive medical history and current symptoms. An appropriate design that aligns with this guideline would be to have these details on the same page, but in different sections with clearly labeled titles. Having these inputs clearly grouped with a legend makes it easy to understand that all fields within a section are related to each other and a single topic. Review a website for the following:

- Related fields should be grouped together visually. Look for visual markers such as borders or background shading that denote groupings
- Review the code by right-clicking on the form and inspecting it. Look for `<fieldset>` tags in the HTML code. Ensure that each group of related fields is enclosed within a `<fieldset>`. Check that each `<fieldset>` contains a `<legend>` tag that provides a meaningful description of the group

Progress Is Displayed Throughout Multi-Page Processes

Clear progress indicators and consistent navigation aids within a process help reduce cognitive load and confusion, making it easier for users to complete complex forms. Aligning a website with this guideline makes it easier for users who may struggle with orientation and navigation due to their disabilities. Review a website as follows:

- Look for a step indicator at the top of the page, clearly marking the current step the user is on
- Look for clearly labeled navigation buttons such as Back and Next or Previous Page and Next Page
- Look for shortcuts or a sidebar menu that allows users to revisit completed sections without losing data entered in subsequent sections

TAB 2: VISIBILITY OF SYSTEM STATUS

The system should always keep users informed about what is going on, through appropriate feedback within a reasonable time. Keep users in the loop and make sure they have the right information quickly. Communicating the current state allows users to feel in control of the system, take appropriate actions to reach their goals, and ultimately trust the brand.

Disabled Fields Are Clearly Discernible from Enabled Fields

Ensuring that users don't have a frustrating experience and abandon their tasks is the primary goal of usability. Adhering to this guideline allows users with visual impairments and color vision deficiency (CVD) to confidently interact with a website's actionable content. Elderly users and those with cognitive disabilities may find it challenging to discern subtle differences in color or shade that indicate a field's status. Relying solely on color to indicate that a UI element is inactive, unusable, or disabled can create frustrating experiences for people. Review a website for:

- Clear contrast between inactive and active form fields
- Text descriptors that indicate a field's status
- Icons or tooltips that appear when a user hovers over or focuses on an inactive field, explaining why it's disabled and what needs to be completed to enable it
- Visual indicators of a field's status, such as additional outlining or other cues to guide the user

Actionable Content Is Obvious

It should be easy to understand what actions can be taken on an element in the UI. Some users, such as those with visual impairments or cognitive disabilities, have trouble recognizing actionable content when it is not clearly marked. Communicating actionable content solely through a color change is not enough. When reviewing a website, look for:

- Underlined in-line text links that are clearly distinguished from the text around them
- Buttons with a 3D appearance or that have a drop shadow to signify actionability
- Hover effects on actionable content, such as changing the cursor to a pointer when users navigate over clickable elements
- Labels on actionable items with larger, bolder fonts that make them stand out from other elements on the page
- Icons associated with labels that explain their action to ensure clarity

Selected Options Are Clearly Indicated with the Help of Highlights

This accessibility guideline helps all users, not just those with disabilities, because it ensures consistent and predictable user experiences. A user interface that clearly differentiates between selected options and options that have not been selected reduces confusion, frustration, and potential errors. To review a website to ensure it adheres to this guideline:

- Look for visual indicators when interacting with navigation menus
- Fill out a form and check for visual indicators for radio inputs (select-one-from-many options), checkboxes (select-many-from-many options), and input fields that are currently selected

Table Sorting: It Is Clear What Is Sortable and What Is Currently Sorted

Clear indicators of sortability and current sort order help users with cognitive disabilities understand the table's organization without needing to remember the interface's state. People with vision impairments benefit from accurately labeled table headers because screen readers can announce sortable content and the current sorting state, which is crucial for understanding how data is organized. The user experience for everyone is significantly degraded when the format in which data is presented is confusing and table views are difficult to manipulate. Ensure a website with sortable table data is accessible:

- Look for table headers that are clickable and visibly distinguished from the content in the table with icons to indicate sortability and the direction of the sort
- Check the code for ARIA attributes that enhance the accessibility of the table, to indicate sort direction on active columns
- Assess what visible feedback is offered in the interface when a column is sorted, such as highlighting the column header

Table Filtering: It Is Clear If a Filter Has Been Applied and What Is Currently Filtered

Similar to sorted table data, filters should be clearly identified and properly labeled to ensure all users understand the results of actions taken. A clear indication of active filters helps maintain context and understanding of the displayed content, reducing confusion and cognitive load. Users with motor disabilities benefit from knowing what filters are applied to avoid unnecessary or repeated interactions. Violating this guideline can result in users unknowingly interacting with content that doesn't meet their needs or expectations, leading to a poor user experience. To check a website for this heuristic:

- Look for a visible update to the interface highlighting active filters when a user applies a filter, such as a different color or a tag that users can easily see and remove
- Check for a summary area where all active filters are listed and can be individually cleared with a single click

There Is Feedback for Meaningful User Interaction

This guideline ensures that users receive immediate and clear confirmation when they interact with UI elements. This can reduce confusion and repeated actions, especially when precision is important. Enhanced feedback can empower older people by giving clear confirmation that they have successfully and correctly interacted with the website. Tactile feedback or larger visual cues can confirm for users with motor disabilities that their selection or interaction was successful. Immediate feedback is crucial for users with cognitive disabilities to confirm that the intended action has taken effect. To identify whether a website gives feedback for meaningful user interaction:

- Look for a distinct visual indicator, such as a border or shadow, when an item is moved or selected
- Look for a progress bar that indicates the status of a form submission
- Listen or feel for a snapping sound or haptic feedback on devices that support it when an item is moved or placed
- Look for a visual indicator such as a confirmation message or notification when an item is placed in a new location or data has been saved

Widget Response Time Is Brief and Provides User Feedback

The response time of on-screen widgets should be approximately less than one second, calculated after the page and its elements have loaded. Providing users with a timely response to interactions is essential to creating a positive, accessible user experience. Delays in response times can cause confusion and hinder understanding, particularly for those who rely on immediate feedback to confirm their actions. When users experience delays, it can lead to multiple clicks, misoperation, and negative emotional responses. Do the following:

- Look for visual indicators such as spinners or progress bars
- Use tools such as Google PageSpeed Insights, Lighthouse, or WebPageTest to analyze the responsiveness of web pages and widgets

What Is a Widget?

In web development, a widget is a small, reusable component or interactive element that serves a specific function or provides specific information on a web page. Widgets can vary widely in functionality and appearance, ranging from simple buttons and forms to more complex elements, such as calendars, maps, weather forecasts, and social media feeds. Here are some common examples of widgets found on websites:

- *Search Bar*: A search widget allows users to enter keywords or phrases to search for specific content within the website
- *Contact Form*: A contact form widget enables users to send messages or inquiries to the website owner or administrator
- *Social Media Buttons*: Social media widgets provide links or buttons that allow users to share content from the website on various social media platforms
- *Weather Forecast*: A weather widget displays current weather conditions and forecasts for a specific location

- *Calendar*: A calendar widget shows upcoming events, appointments, or important dates
- *Chatbot*: A chatbot widget provides an interactive chat interface that allows users to ask questions or seek assistance from a virtual assistant
- *Shopping Cart*: A shopping cart widget displays the items selected by the user for purchase and allows them to proceed to checkout
- *Video Player*: A video widget embeds a video player on the web page, allowing users to watch videos without leaving the site
- *Newsletter Signup Form*: A newsletter signup widget collects user email addresses for subscribing to newsletters or updates from the website
- *Polls and Surveys*: Poll or survey widgets enable users to participate in polls or surveys directly on the website

Processes Over Two Seconds Show Progress

Similar to the expectations for widgets to respond to user input or action within one second, all website processes should communicate to the user that the system is taking action. Uncertainty about process duration and completion of processes contributes to anxiety disorders. Giving users visual cues such as progress bars reassures all users that the process is ongoing and allows them to gauge its duration. Clear progress indicators help manage expectations. To review how well a website adheres to this criterion:

- Look for visual indications that a process is ongoing. This could be a spinning loader animation, a visual bar that fills up as progress is made, a percentage indicator, or textual clues indicating the time remaining
- Assess interactions with a screen reader to listen for progress updates

TAB 3: CONTENT CLARITY AND READABILITY

On tab 3 of the spreadsheet, we're reviewing a website to make sure that information is presented using the appropriate medium and is tailored to the user's level of understanding.

Form Field Labels Are Arranged in a Readable Vertical Format

Keeping text in a standard, predictable layout makes it easier for humans to process information quickly. Rotated or angled text can be challenging to read for elderly users, users with visual impairments, and those with cognitive disabilities. A website that does not align with this guideline can lead to increased errors in form completion, user frustration, and task abandonment. Review a website:

- Look for form fields and ensure they are not angled or positioned in a way that impacts accessibility
- Check that form field labels are clear and use high-contrast text

Obvious Distinctions Are Made Between Choose One and Choose Many Options

It should be obvious to users what the expected input should be for a form field requiring them to select one or many options. Typically, a form field where the user can choose one of many options is a radio button style. Where a user can make several selections from many options, a checkbox input type is appropriate. Review the website for adherence to this criterion:

- Look for select-one-of-many form inputs and ensure that the radio style selection is clear and obvious
- Look for select-many-of-many form inputs and ensure that the checkbox style selection is clear and obvious
- Review the code and ensure that the appropriate HTML input types are assigned to the form inputs

The Website Uses Font Sizes That Are Large Enough to Be Comfortably Read on Standard Displays

To ensure information is clear for all users, regardless of ability, the minimum body text size on a website should be at least 16 pixels. Text smaller than 16 pixels can be difficult for many people to read, especially on screens with high resolution or for users with visual impairments. Modern web browsers and devices are optimized for text sizes around 16 pixels, providing a good balance between legibility and aesthetics. Larger text improves the overall user experience by reducing eye strain and making content more accessible. To assess whether a website meets this heuristic:

- Use browser developer tools to inspect the text size of different sections, particularly paragraphs and non-heading text
- Check that the font size of the body text is set to at least 16 pixels

- Use automated tools and accessibility checkers to highlight instances where text size falls below this threshold

The Website Uses Larger Font Sizes for Metrics and Data

Important information should always be larger, not smaller, than the labels for the important information. Review the website for this heuristic:

- Use browser developer tools to inspect the text size of metrics and other important data points
- Look for a distinct difference in font size, color, and weight that distinguishes metrics and data from body text

Dates Are Clear for All Users, Including International Users

Standardizing date formats or clearly indicating the format used (e.g., DD/MM/YYYY vs. MM/DD/YYYY) prevents confusion and errors, particularly in global contexts where date formats vary widely. Clear and consistent presentation of dates helps those with cognitive disabilities as well as elderly users and those with temporary impairments. Violating this guideline can result in users misinterpreting dates, which can be critical in contexts such as booking tickets, submitting applications, or fulfilling deadlines, leading to missed opportunities or serious inconveniences. Check a website for this:

- Look for clearly labeled date formats next to date entry fields using an unambiguous example (e.g., Format: Month (MM), Day (DD), Year (YYYY))
- Check for features that allow users to select their preferred date format from a list or that automatically adjust date formats based on the user's location
- Check for tooltips or a help link that explains the date format with examples from various locations
- Check all instances in the interface where a date is presented or requested to ensure the format is clearly labeled or adjustable

Metrics Are Labeled Clearly, with Detailed Information About the Data Easily Available as Needed

Ensure that all content, especially quantitative data, is accessible to all users. Properly labeled data and easy access to detailed explanations are critical to make sure that users, regardless of their level of technical or cognitive abilities, can understand the provided metrics. Elderly users or those with cognitive disabilities may find it easier to understand complex information and interact with the website effectively when data is appropriately presented. Users with visual impairments rely on clearly labeled data to be announced by screen readers, particularly for non-text content such as graphs or charts. To make sure a website aligns with this criterion:

- Review the website for clear, plain-language labels alongside critical data

- Look for tooltips or help icons next to metrics that, when hovered over or selected, provide a simple explanation of the data and how it should be interpreted

- Check for links to a glossary or help page where users can get more detailed information about the metrics and terms used

TAB 4: USER CONTROL AND FREEDOM

Informed Choices: The Consequences of Actions a User Can Take Are Communicated Clearly

Users should be able to make informed decisions based on a clear understanding of the implications and potential outcomes of their actions. A website can avoid user confusion and potential frustration by communicating the consequences of actions. Not following this guideline can lead to unintended actions, such as submitting incomplete or incorrect forms, leading to potential financial or legal repercussions. This can be especially damaging for vulnerable populations. Review a website for this heuristic:

- Look for confirmation steps in a process where users can review their choices along with a detailed summary of the potential impact

- Check the interface for clear descriptions in the immediate vicinity of each choice outlining potential risks and outcomes

- Look for tooltips or contextual icons that users can hover over or select to get more information about specific actions or options

- Look for visual cues, such as color coding, that indicate the severity or impact of a choice

In the Context of a Multi-Step User Flow, the User Can Go Back to Previous Steps and Make Changes

Following this guideline ensures that users can navigate and interact with a website without confusion. All users benefit from being able to review and correct actions and selections made in previous steps. This helps people understand complex processes and reduces cognitive load. Assess a website for the following:

- Breadcrumbs or a progress bar should indicate where a user is in a workflow or process
- Data should be saved when navigating between pages in a process
- Navigation should be available to move between pages, such as Next and Previous buttons

Users Can Cancel an Operation in Progress and Be Returned to the Immediate Point from Where They Started Within the Process

Allow users to maintain control over their interactions with a website. Users with cognitive disabilities might start an action and realize partway through that they misunderstood the requirements or consequences. Users with motor impairments might accidentally initiate a process due to fine motor control challenges. Users who might be distracted or under stress benefit from being able to easily cancel actions they start by mistake. Being able to cancel an action or process helps prevent errors and reduces user frustration. To ensure a website aligns with this criterion:

- Look for a Cancel button that stops a process or transaction at any point before the final submission
- Review a process for a final confirmation step where users can review and edit details before submitting

Users Are Prompted to Confirm Commands That Have Destructive Consequences

Users benefit from additional confirmation and clear warnings about destructive actions and irreversible choices to help them understand the consequences. Users with dexterity issues might accidentally activate buttons; thus, a confirmation dialog can help prevent unintended actions. People with visual impairments and cognitive disabilities often benefit from additional confirmations and clear warnings, ensuring they are fully aware of the actions they are about to take. Violations of this guideline can lead to unintended consequences, such as deleting data, incurring additional costs, or overlooked details. This can lead to user distress, dissatisfaction, and potential legal issues. Review the website for the following:

- Look for confirmation dialogs that clearly state the consequences of taking an action and ask for explicit user confirmation
- Check for a secondary step in a process to confirm the action, such as the user typing DELETE or a code to ensure they understand the permanent outcome of the action taken
- Assess the website for visual and auditory alerts that employ strong colors (such as red for warnings) and auditory cues (for screen reader users) to indicate the severity of the action

Users Can Easily Undo an Action

This guideline is vital for making digital environments accessible and forgiving, and particularly benefits users with motor impairments, cognitive disabilities, and visual impairments. Users may make unintended selections or entries and need the ability to easily correct these without penalty. When reviewing a website, look for the following:

- Look for an Undo button featured prominently on the interface
- Check that the undo feature can be activated via keyboard shortcuts and is accessible through assistive technologies
- Look for a confirmation message or tooltip that confirms the last action has been undone

Users Can Easily Redo an Action

Ensure that website interfaces are accessible and user-friendly by making it possible for users to change their mind or providing a simple way to revert changes when they make a mistake. Review a website for this heuristic:

- Check that standard keyboard shortcuts are available and functional, such as Ctrl+Z for undo and Ctrl+Shift+Z for redo
- Look for accessible undo and redo buttons in the website toolbar
- Use a screen reader and check that auditory feedback is given when actions are undone or redone

User-Created Data Can Be Changed or Deleted

Users may need to correct mistakes or change their mind about the data they have input. Users with difficulty making precise movements benefit from being able to easily correct mistakes. People with visual impairments need interface elements that allow them to edit and delete data entered. All users need to be able to correct incorrectly entered data with straightforward mechanisms. Check a website for this heuristic:

- Ensure clear icons and text labels are in close proximity to edit and delete options and are accessible via keyboard shortcuts
- Look for confirmation dialogs that are simple to understand and interact with, reducing the risk of accidentally deleting data

TAB 5: CONSISTENCY AND STANDARDS

Most Important Information Is First or Near the Beginning of the Page

Placing the most important information first on the page helps users quickly understand the main purpose of the page without being overwhelmed by less critical content. For users relying on screen readers, having crucial information first reduces the time and effort needed to find relevant content. Older people have reduced cognitive flexibility and benefit from straightforward content presentation where key information is easily accessible. Not following this guideline can lead to a poor user experience that particularly impacts those who rely on a logical and efficient presentation of content to navigate effectively. When reviewing a website:

- Look for a logical presentation of essential information on each page
- Examine the structure of web pages to ensure the most critical features are presented first or near the top of the page
- Check whether the layout remains logical and information is appropriately prioritized across different devices and screen sizes

Icons Used Follow a Design Scheme That Is Consistent Across the Website

Consistency in icon design isn't just for visual effect; it helps users to more easily recognize and understand the function of icons and related features. Older users and those with temporary impairments (such as people experiencing temporary visual strain) will find a consistent icon scheme easier to navigate, minimizing the cognitive effort required to relearn different icon designs. Review a website to see how it aligns with this heuristic:

- Look for text labels adjacent to or near icons that enhance understanding
- Check for visual consistency and uniformity in icon style, color, and size

Field Labels Are Left-Justified and to the Left of the Input Field or Above It

The consistent and predictable placement of field labels helps users understand and remember how to interact with forms, reducing cognitive load and confusion. For languages that read from left to right, form labels should always be left-justified and positioned to the left or directly above the form input field. Review the website for the following:

- Check all forms on the website to ensure field labels are consistently placed to the left or above the fields

Selected Colors Are Consistent with Common Expectations About Communicating with Color

This principle ensures that users can easily perceive the information presented on the website. This guideline is particularly important for users with CVD to understand content when color is used to convey information, as they might rely on these commonly understood color codes and process information based on how those colors appear to them. Using color codes that align with common expectations helps all users, including those with cognitive disabilities, to understand the information quickly and accurately. This guideline also assists users with color blindness by providing a consistent and familiar color scheme. Do the following when reviewing a website:

- Check the website's use of color to ensure it aligns with common expectations, such as using red for errors or destructive actions, yellow for warnings or important alerts, and green for confirmation or successful actions

Titles and Labels Are Semantically Consistent

Users with cognitive and learning disabilities rely on consistent grammar to understand a website's content. Text in the UI should consistently refer to the user from the same point of view (i.e., My jobs vs.

Your jobs). Users can experience confusion and frustration if sections of content change grammatically without warning. Do the following:

- Review titles and labels to ensure they are grammatically consistent across all pages of the website
- Review content for a consistent point of view

Numbers, Currency, and Symbols Are Shown Consistently Across the System

Consistently using numbers, currency, and symbols across a website will primarily benefit users with cognitive impairments who rely on consistency to understand and compare numerical data. Any user could be confused if numbers, currency, and symbols are displayed inconsistently, which could lead to the misinterpretation of data. Do the following:

- Look for instances where numbers, currency, and symbols are used across pages of the website and verify they are displayed in the same format

TAB 6: RECOGNITION RATHER THAN RECALL

Consistent Use of Visual and Text Prompts

Visual cues and prompts should be displayed in consistent and obvious places. Many users will benefit from consistency in both the location and appearance of prompts, including high contrast and simple text. Visually impaired users who rely on screen readers or magnification will benefit from predictable locations for prompts so they can easily find these elements. Interfaces that align with this criterion will reduce user errors and frustration. Assess a website for this:

- Navigate the website and look for messages and prompts communicating errors or help to users
- Systematically document the location and appearance of these notifications, alerts, and prompts
- Look for visual cues that distinguish these elements from the content around them and conform to a standard style

Main Icons Are Easily Remembered After Initial Experience

Consistent and memorable icons help users navigate and understand website features without needing to relearn the interface each time they visit. Recognizable icons, when paired with appropriate text alternatives, aid those using screen readers by providing consistent navigation clues across visits. For elderly users, familiar icons reduce cognitive load and make digital environments less intimidating. Review the website interface:

- Examine icons used across the website to ensure they are visually distinct and consistently placed
- Check whether accessible names are assigned via ARIA labels or alt text

Icons That Are Custom to the Product Are Consistently Used

All users can benefit from the consistent use, style, and placement of custom icons. This helps users understand and remember the functionalities associated with each icon, reducing cognitive load and facilitating ease of navigation. Do the following:

- Check all pages of the website for the consistent use, style, and placement of custom icons
- Ensure that icons that are used for the same function appear identical across the website
- Verify that text alternatives are provided for each icon

Icons That Are Less Familiar Have Labels Near the Icons

Text labels help users understand the purpose of icons that are not immediately recognizable, facilitating better comprehension and navigation. Do the following:

- Examine icons used throughout the website to ensure that each is accompanied by a clear and descriptive label or has a hover-text feature
- Check that labels are accessible to screen readers and visible to all users

TAB 7: FLEXIBILITY AND EFFICIENCY OF USE

Accelerators, or "shortcuts"—not known by the novice user—may speed up the interaction for the expert user such that the system can cater to both inexperienced and experienced users. Allow users to tailor frequent actions. Make it easy for users to accelerate to their desired destination or goal. The system supports multiple levels of user expertise by providing an experience that supports both novices and advanced users.

For All Transaction Sequences, All Required Data Is Obviously Marked for the User

The clear presentation of required data helps users understand what is expected without needing to remember instructions from previous pages or other sections of the website. This reduces potential errors and facilitates smoother transactions. Users should be aware of all needed data as it aids in comprehension and task completion, especially in complex transaction sequences. Review the website for this heuristic:

- Check forms for required field indicators
- Review forms for logical information grouping
- Look for tooltips and inline validation messages that provide immediate guidance if the user enters incorrect information

Users Are Not Asked for Too Much Information, or More Than the Bare Minimum for the Task at Hand

While this guideline is primarily assessing for a usability issue, asking for more information than is absolutely necessary also impacts accessibility. Users with limited dexterity, visual impairments, or cognitive disabilities may feel overwhelmed by lengthy forms and find it challenging to complete them. Many users find it intrusive to be asked to submit information that isn't directly relevant to the task at hand, impacting trust in the brand and website. Assess a website for compliance with this guideline:

- Review all forms on the website and check for the number of required fields
- Ensure all form fields are necessary for the task at hand
- Check that all optional fields are clearly marked

Users Are Able to Customize Information, Selections, or Views to Suit Their Needs

Whenever possible, content should be adaptable by the user to meet their needs and increase the benefit they get from the website. Users with low vision or color blindness benefit from the ability to customize color contrasts and text sizes to make the content more readable. Users with cognitive impairments, such as dyslexia, can customize text spacing and font styles to enhance readability. Users with limited dexterity can benefit from customizable input methods, larger target sizes, and adjustable interface elements to reduce physical strain. Review a website for compliance with this guideline:

- Check for the presence of customization options for text size, color contrast, and spacing
- Look for options for color scheme and dark mode/light mode
- Check for grid view vs. list view options for layout
- Check for language drop-down selection menus
- Assess whether the website has a dashboard feature where users can customize what information they see
- Look for content filtering options
- Check for customizable notifications
- For videos, look for options to adjust the playback speed

The System Supports Accelerators, Such as Keyboard Shortcuts

Keyboard shortcuts allow experienced users who are proficient with technology to efficiently access the information they need, without detracting from the experience of new users. Individuals who cannot use a mouse due to motor disabilities or temporary space limitations benefit from being able to navigate quickly between sections and actions via the keyboard. Look for the following to make sure a website is compliant with this heuristic:

- Navigate through the website to ensure all functions can be used by keyboard interactions alone
- Manually test the website for common keyboard shortcuts, such as Ctrl+S for Save, Ctrl+O for Open, and Ctrl+C for Copy

Information Is Filled in for the User as Much as Possible

This guideline focuses on helping users avoid and correct mistakes by making interactions more forgiving and providing support where needed. Pre-filling information can significantly help users who struggle with memory or decision-making by reducing the amount of new information they need to process and recall. Complex forms are made easier to fill out when previously known information is pre-filled for users. For example, on a healthcare portal website the form might have basic details such as name, insurance information, height, and even recurring health data already filled in. The user is prompted to confirm and update information, reducing the time spent on forms and decreasing the error rate, significantly improving compliance with necessary health monitoring and increasing patient satisfaction. Review a website for this guideline:

- Evaluate how the website handles user data across sessions
- Check whether the website appropriately pre-fills information where possible and ensures data accuracy and security

TAB 8: AESTHETIC AND MINIMALIST DESIGN

Interfaces should not contain information that is irrelevant or rarely needed. The visual design of a website should reinforce the purpose of the page using the minimum necessary elements. Visual clutter and irrelevant information should be eliminated. Every extra unit of information in a dialog competes with relevant units of information and diminishes their relative visibility.

Headings Are Brief, Yet Long Enough to Communicate

This guideline ensures that web content is organized and easy to navigate, particularly for users who rely on assistive technologies. Well-structured titles and headings improve the usability and accessibility of web pages, making it easier for users to find and understand the information they need. For example, organizing a frequently asked questions (FAQ) page with clear, brief headings such as Shipping and Returns instead of Information about Shipping Policies and Details on How to Return Items provides a cleaner and more navigable structure. Review a website for this heuristic:

- Review each page's title and headings to ensure they are concise yet descriptive enough to communicate the content of the page effectively
- Check that headings are used consistently and appropriately to organize content

The Interface Is Uncluttered, and Contains No (or Minimal) Decorative Elements

Information needs to be presented in ways that are perceptible and obvious to all users. Minimizing the decorative elements on a web page helps users focus on essential content without being distracted.

Simplified interfaces help users complete tasks faster and enhance readability. These decorative features, such as script-style display fonts, using multiple styles of fonts on one page, and adding many non-essential graphics, add to the cognitive load for users. This can cause users to feel frustrated and overwhelmed and can contribute to task abandonment. Assess a website for this guideline:

- Review the style and design elements used on a website. Assess the balance between necessary content and decorative elements to ensure clarity and focus are maintained

- Review all decorative elements and ensure they have empty alt text (alt="") so that screen readers can ignore them

Content Is Brief and Concise, Providing Enough Information for Users to Understand What Actions to Take

This guideline can be subjective and entirely dependent on the context of the website. Primarily, adhering to this guideline requires reducing long-winded descriptions and complex language that users might find confusing. By employing concise language and clear instructions, and only sharing additional information if requested by users, a website can enhance the user experience and increase success rates for user tasks. Do the following:

- Review all instructions and descriptions for clarity and conciseness

- Look for opportunities to leverage progressive disclosure in the context of complex forms or tasks

Content Is Prioritized to Support User Goals

Information on a website should be presented to the user in a meaningful sequence. The effective organization and prioritization of content assists those using assistive technologies such as screen readers to focus on relevant information without being distracted or overwhelmed by less important details. Reducing the number of popups, ads, interruptive notifications, and promotional banners makes the user experience better and can improve task performance and website loading times. Assess a website for this criterion:

- Evaluate the website to ensure that, on each page, the most important content is prominently displayed and aligns with user goals

- Check whether the content hierarchy is logical and facilitates easy navigation

TAB 9: ERROR PREVENTION AND RECOVERY

Good error messages are important, but the best designs carefully prevent problems from occurring in the first place. The design of a system provides sufficient safeguards to keep the user from making mistakes within a page or across an application.

Required Format Shown When Users Need to Enter Information Formatted Specifically

This guideline ensures that users are given clear instructions when they need to enter information in a specific format. This prevents errors and enhances the user experience by reducing frustration and confusion. Many users struggle when expected to remember format requirements, making filling out forms a frustrating task. Clear instructions help them enter information correctly the first time and enhance the overall user experience. Users who rely on screen readers need format instructions to be read aloud. If the format is not specified, they may enter data incorrectly. Users with limited dexterity may find it difficult to correct errors. When reviewing forms on a website:

- Look for placeholder text in the input fields that defines the format required (e.g., MM/DD/YYYY for date of birth or XXXX-XXXX-XXXX-XXXX for credit card number)
- Look for instructions in close proximity to the input fields (e.g., Enter your phone number in the format (123) 456-7890)

Forms Give a Clear Indication of the Number of Character Spaces Available in a Field

This guideline ensures that users are aware of the constraints and requirements for input fields, which helps them provide the correct type and length of information. It prevents users from encountering errors after inputting data, enhancing the UX and reducing frustration. Users benefit from knowing the constraints of the form field in advance, as it reduces the need for corrections and unnecessary rework. When assessing a website:

- Look for clearly stated character limits for the form field where limits apply either within the input field as placeholder text or as a label above or below the field
- Check for character counters that update as the user types, showing how many characters they have used and how many they have left

The System Warns Users When They're About to Make a Potentially Serious Error

This guideline ensures that users are warned before making potentially serious errors, such as submitting incorrect data that could result in financial loss, legal commitments, or other significant consequences. Some users may struggle to notice or correct errors without explicit warnings, leading to unintended consequences. Look for this guideline on a website:

- Check for the potential for serious errors on the website, such as forms involving financial transactions, legal commitments, or data deletion
- Review the presence of summary pages, confirmation pages, or dialog boxes before final submissions
- Look for highlighted errors in forms or on confirmation pages
- Check for banner notifications for errors
- Look for real-time validation systems that check things such as credit card numbers, proper address formatting, and phone numbers, and notify the user to correct any errors before submission

Errors and Informational Messages Have a Link for More Details When Appropriate

When users receive adequate information, they are more likely to understand and correct errors. Providing a link for "more details" allows users to access further explanations or steps to resolve issues, which is particularly helpful for complex errors, multi-stage problems, or informational messages that require further context. Users benefit from clear, detailed instructions that they can follow to fix errors or take correct actions. It's appropriate to include an error code in an error message; however, more detail is necessary to ensure the user understands the meaning of the error code and what to do about it. An example would be for a job application form where a start date and end date are required. If entered in the wrong format, a brief error message might state Invalid date format, but without additional details, the user may not know the correct format. Linking to a page, tooltip, or modal dialog explaining the acceptable date format ensures the form is filled out completely and accurately. Review a website for this guideline:

- Check whether all error and informational messages include links for more details where appropriate

- Review the content linked to ensure it provides comprehensive and clear instructions for solving issues

Error Messages Use Consistent and Traditional Grammatical Style, Form, Terminology, and Abbreviations

Making content understandable to most users requires simplifying the language to reach the broadest possible audience. People with cognitive disabilities or learning difficulties may struggle with complex language or inconsistent terminology, which can confuse them when encountering errors. Non-native speakers may be particularly sensitive to complicated phrasing or inconsistent use of terms, which could make navigating error messages more challenging. Visually impaired users or users with temporary impairments, such as someone in a distracting environment, need clear instructions to efficiently resolve errors without additional cognitive load. Assess a website for compliance:

- Review all error messages across the website for consistency in language and style. This could be done manually or with the help of automated tools that scan for text patterns

Error Messages Are Clearly Worded and Use the Normal Action-Object Syntax Consistently

Clear and consistent error messages are crucial for helping users understand what went wrong and how to fix it. Using normal action-object syntax makes the instructions more intuitive and easier to follow. For example, consider a user who is completing an online registration form and forgets to fill out a mandatory field. Upon attempting to submit the form, an error message pops up. If the message consistently uses a clear action-object format (e.g., "Enter your age in the Age field"), it directly guides the user on what to do next, as opposed to a more ambiguous or variably structured message (e.g., Age needs entry), which might confuse the user. Check a website for adherence to this guideline:

- Check all error messages for clarity and consistency
- Ensure error messages follow the normal action-object syntax

Error Messages Suggest the Cause and Solution to the Problem

The guidelines for web content accessibility suggest that if an error is automatically detected and suggestions for correction are known, then the suggestions should be provided to the user. Providing thorough and meaningful error messages that suggest the cause and provide solutions to the problem improves the user experience and reduces frustration. For example, in an online checkout form, if a user makes a mistake entering their credit card number, an error message saying Invalid input is too vague and unhelpful. A better error message could be one that says "The credit card number you entered is invalid. Please enter a 16-digit credit card number without spaces or dashes." Review a website for this heuristic:

- Look for error messages that explain what the problem is
- Verify that error messages provide specific instructions on how to correct the error

Prompts Are Clear and Concise, Providing Preventive Measures to Be Taken

Communication with users is most effective when it includes straight-forward instructions that reduce cognitive load and prevent mistakes before they happen. Forms that provide concise prompts that use plain language significantly improve the user experience, building trust with customers. Examples might include tooltips or additional information icons next to fields where users typically make mistakes, such as entering a date of birth in the wrong format. Tooltips can clearly explain the expected format and provide an example. This aids users in completing the form correctly on the first attempt. Assess a website for this:

- Review prompts for proactive help in context with form fields
- Check that form fields have in-line validation
- Look for icons or graphics that visually complement text instructions

Prompts Are Expressed in Plain Language with No Error Codes or Jargon

Proactively preventing misunderstandings, user errors, and abandonment of tasks is essential for a positive user experience. Most users, including those who depend on screen readers and users with cognitive disabilities, benefit from plain language prompts that don't contain error codes, complex instructions, or technical jargon. Review a website for adherence to this criterion:

- Check prompts for how clearly they are worded and that they don't include error codes or technical language

TAB 10: HELP AND DOCUMENTATION

Even though it is better if the system can be used without documentation, it may be necessary to provide help and documentation. Any such information should be easy to search for, be focused on the user's task, list concrete steps to be carried out, and not be too large.

The Help System Interface Is Consistent with the Navigation, Presentation, and Conversation Interfaces of the Application It Supports

This guideline ensures a consistent and intuitive UX, especially for users with cognitive or learning disabilities, or those who rely on assistive technologies. Inconsistent help systems can lead to confusion, frustration, and potential errors, making it difficult for users to effectively utilize the available support resources. If the help system interface (navigation, presentation, and conversation) is inconsistent with the main website interface, users may become confused and struggle to find the appropriate support resources. This can be particularly problematic for users with cognitive or learning disabilities, as well as those using screen readers, who rely on consistent interfaces to understand and navigate the available help resources effectively. To assess a website's interface for consistent help:

- Identify context-sensitive help resources (e.g., tooltips, popups, and help sections) that are available throughout the website
- Check that the navigation is consistent with the main website
- Verify that the visual presentation of information is aligned with the layout, styling, and typography of the main website
- If the help system includes conversational elements (e.g., chatbots or virtual assistants), ensure that the language, tone, and interaction patterns are consistent with the main website

Assistive Documentation Is Easy to Find and Search, and Is Offered in the Context of the Tasks the User Is Trying to Complete

Websites that follow this guideline ensure that users, particularly those with disabilities or impairments, can easily access and understand the available help resources within a website or application. Failure to provide accessible and context-sensitive help can lead to frustration, confusion, and potential errors, hindering the user's ability to complete tasks or fully utilize the website's features. Review a website for adherence to this guideline:

- Look at all pages of the website for clearly marked indications of help resources in the context of the task at hand
- Review the ease of use for finding specific resources or assistance by searching the documentation

Assistive Documentation Offers Concrete Steps That Users Can Follow to Complete Their Tasks

Ensure all users, particularly those with disabilities or impairments, can access and understand the instructional documentation provided within a website. Clear and comprehensive instructions can significantly improve the user experience and enable users to be self-sufficient as they navigate and interact with the website's features and content. If the instructional documentation lacks clarity or completeness, or fails to provide concrete steps for users to follow, individuals with disabilities or impairments may struggle to understand and complete the necessary tasks within the website. This can lead to frustration, errors, and potential abandonment of the website. Review a website for this:

- Look for instructional documentation in the form of step-by-step guides, tutorials, contextual help panels, video tutorials, and FAQs
- Check all instructional documentation for clarity and completeness

Users Can Start Work Where They Left Off After Accessing Help and Switch Back to Help Again Easily, If Required

This guideline ensures that users have a streamlined experience using the website, including accessing any assistive documentation needed to support their tasks. This is important because it ensures that users can efficiently resume their tasks after seeking help without losing their progress. This feature is essential for maintaining task flow and reducing frustration, especially for users with disabilities. Assess the website for the following:

- Navigate through the website to check whether tasks can be paused and resumed without losing progress
- Ensure that accessing help documentation does not disrupt the user's workflow

Congratulations! We've made it through every checklist item on our website evaluation spreadsheet. Time for a break. In the next chapter, we'll assess our findings and collect the most important information to present to stakeholders.

CHAPTER 5

SYNTHESIZE AND RECOMMEND

If the previous chapter felt like a hefty tome, this one should feel more like a refreshing short story. The hardest part is evaluating the website against WCAG and documenting our findings. In this chapter, we'll discuss how to assess the results of the website evaluation and make recommendations that will positively impact the business.

ASSESSMENT RESULTS

What do we know now that we've looked at the whole website? The evaluation of a website can be done over time, over multiple sessions. Typically, the assessment takes place at least a day after the evaluation has been completed. It's helpful to return to the spreadsheet with "fresh eyes" that haven't been "zoomed in" and focused on looking for specific criteria.

Automated Tools

There are additional automated tools we can use to supplement our manual evaluation. Some of the most popular and well supported include:

- WAVE Accessibility Evaluation Tool by WebAIM: Available as a browser extension for Chrome, Firefox, and Microsoft Edge. It provides an overlay of icons indicating potential accessibility issues on a web page.

- axe DevTools by Deque: A Chrome extension that analyzes a web page for accessibility defects and provides guidance on how to fix them.
- Accessibility Insights for Web by Microsoft: A browser extension that includes automated checks, visualizing tab stops, and a guide for manual assessments. It can also save accessibility reports.
- ANDI (Accessible Name & Description Inspector): A "favelet" or "bookmarklet" that provides automated detection of accessibility issues, reveals what a screen reader should say for interactive elements, and offers practical suggestions.
- UX Check: A Chrome extension that helps identify and annotate usability issues according to Nielsen's 10 usability heuristics. Can be customized with company-specific heuristics.

These tools can automatically scan a website's code and content, flagging potential accessibility issues based on WCAG. It's important to note, however, that while automated tools are helpful, they cannot catch every error or evaluate content quality. That's why most professionals working in accessibility will always suggest a manual evaluation, such as the checklist we used in the last chapter. Additional manual testing is recommended for a comprehensive accessibility evaluation, including screen reader reviews and user testing with individuals with disabilities.

SUMMARY TAB

Let's first take a look at the Summary tab of the spreadsheet.

Evaluation Details

First, we can update some information to track our efforts: to the right side of this page is the Evaluation Details panel. Here are details meant to be filled in by the evaluator(s) of the website. Add their name(s) and the date the evaluation was completed. If it took place over several days, it's okay to just put the final date. At the bottom of this panel, it's best practice to denote the browser, device, and operating system, but this information can be left off and not impact the outcome.

Below the evaluator information is a legend for the text colors used in the two main sections that depict the impact on the user experience. These are useful as a quick way to identify the lowest usability and accessibility scores at a glance.

Score Legend

0 = Usability catastrophe

1 = Major usability disruption

2 = Disruptive user experience

3 = Cosmetic problems; no negative impact

4 = Positive user experience

The closer a score is to 0, the worse the user experience is. The color codes of the spreadsheet correspond to common color expectations about positive experiences (green) and negative experiences (red). These are intended to give the eye something to gravitate toward when looking for the most impactful issues to focus on.

Evaluation Scores

Also on this page are two main sections with scores populated on the right side of each section. At the top, we have a Usability evaluation score for [website]. Update the information in brackets with the name of the website or the URL.

Below Usability evaluation score, we see Accessibility evaluation score. Both of these main sections provide "roll up" scores for the individual topics. Usability evaluation score populates a total score for each tab, and Accessibility evaluation score populates a total score for each section of the Accessibility tab.

Scores Above 3

If you've reviewed the website and none of the roll-up scores are lower than 3, then this might not be a viable candidate website for a redesign. According to the parameters of this evaluation, the website has cosmetic issues only, with very few accessibility or usability issues. That's fantastic news! This evaluation process does not, however, consider the visual design of the website. There may be value you can bring to the aesthetic design of the website that has nothing to do with accessibility or usability. It's up to you to determine whether this project is worth pursuing for gaining practical UX experience.

IDENTIFY MUST-FIX ISSUES

To start the information synthesis process, consider: What tabs have the lowest scores? Let's take a look at those first. Click the link to revisit a tab and make a note on a separate sheet of any criterion that has a score of Never or Rarely or that has any priority assigned to it. Remember, we only assigned a priority for really major issues, so even if the priority assigned was low, it was still enough of a priority to be marked as important.

Once you have re-visited all tabs of the evaluation spreadsheet and made notes of all the low-scoring issues, you might also take a look at the criteria that scored at a medium level, the ones marked as Sometimes. Are any of these meaningful enough to add to the list?

Looking at a list doesn't help us identify patterns, so we're going to use a UX research method to process the data more effectively: an affinity diagram. You will need to use sticky notes, either with actual sticky notes or online versions using FigJam, Miro, or another whiteboard design tool. There should be one sticky note per data point. Distinguish sticky notes based on the score, if possible—red or dark pink sticky notes for Never scores and orange sticky notes for Rarely scores. Alternatively, use a theme based on the colors of sticky notes that you have available. This is just for your benefit to find patterns in the severity of issues.

If the data generated from this analysis seems like an overwhelming amount, don't worry; that's normal. We often need to sift through enormous amounts of incomplete or confusing information when we're looking for what we consider "statistically significant" data.

After creating a sticky note for each data point, start clustering them by theme or relatedness, just like creating an affinity diagram after conducting user interviews. Take some time to arrange these sticky notes from a large pile into clusters of more nuanced themes. Depending on how many sticky notes you have created, this could take 45 minutes to a couple of hours. Some sticky notes might seem related because of the usability heuristic they were grouped by in the spreadsheet, but consider relationships between types of content, pages of the website, user tasks, and phases of the experience (browsing, purchasing or booking, etc.).

Once all sticky notes have been sorted, consider how you have categorized them. Were certain heuristics violated more frequently than others? Were those heuristics linked to specific types of UI elements, content, or user actions? What information can we derive from these details?

Remember, this website evaluation isn't meant to turn up every issue that could possibly be found on the website. We're looking for meaningful problems that we can bring to the stakeholders that will help us convince them to let us fix them. This skill is one you build over time, by practicing this process. It does get easier.

This instruction might seem vague, but like most things in UX—it depends. The results you find will depend entirely on the website you've evaluated. Keep in mind that we're looking for between 3 and 9 meaningful issues that impact accessibility for users or add friction to the user experience.

Pull out the top 10 things that you think are the most important to fix. We'll focus on these to make recommendations.

PRIORITIZE THE ISSUES AND MAKE RECOMMENDATIONS

After we've identified the issues that are creating friction in the user experience or preventing people from using the website, we want to bring our recommendations to stakeholders. We don't want to overwhelm them with hundreds of tiny things that need to be addressed, however—just the essentials.

The long list of small fixes is what we're keeping to refer back to when we're updating the website. First, we have to convince the stakeholders that fixing the website is necessary. To do that, we've got to show that we can make an impact on their business in specific ways.

Prioritize High-Impact Problems

Up to this point, we have just been collecting the "worst" issues we find and gathering them in one place to get a big-picture idea of what we need to fix. We do that by focusing on the accessibility issues first.

Can you identify just three problems that impact accessibility? These are the top-priority issues to bring to the stakeholders. The notes you've made on the Accessibility tab should make these issues clear. Refine related issues into one streamlined statement to communicate with the stakeholders.

Describe the fixes you would make in simple language, explaining why they will improve the accessibility of the website or simplify the user experience. Let's review a few examples.

Example 1: Beauty Services

On a beauty services website, the biggest problems found on the Accessibility tab had to do with navigation and wayfinding, visual and auditory alternatives, and language and readability. Let's review some of the issues found that were marked as Rarely or Never.

Navigation and Wayfinding:

- Pages don't have meaningful title text
- A skip link is not provided on any page
- Navigation has a lot of options and no apparent priority
- Pages don't use section headings

Language and Readability:

- The content hierarchy does not use multiple levels of headings
- Content is not designed using short blocks of text
- Important points are not formatted into lists

Visual and Auditory Alternatives:

- Informative images do not have meaningful alt text (alt text is very close or identical to image name)
- Decorative images are not identified by empty alt tags

Without looking at any other page in the spreadsheet, we know that this website has some accessibility issues that make it difficult for people using assistive technology to effectively interact with the website. These issues might be the focus of the presentation to the stakeholders.

We might say that the top 3 opportunities for the beauty website could be:

1. Make it easy for users to find what they need. Streamlining the navigation and adding a "skip link" for accessibility will significantly improve this. Adding meaningful page title text and adding section headings to guide the user will make navigation and wayfinding better for users.

2. Refine the content for users to scan quickly. There's a lot of information available, but it's difficult to read and most users will scan it but not read it in depth. Without an appropriate hierarchy, the details users need in order to feel comfortable booking a service are lost.

3. Add alt text to all images. Users need more information to feel confident booking expensive beauty services. Provide the right details by adding meaningful alt text to all images. This will enhance the striking before-and-after shots that show off the skills of the stakeholders.

Additional suggestions can be added to this priority list that support these efforts, but we'll talk about "reading the room" in the next chapter. For now, aim for enough information to convince the stakeholders but not so much that they'll shut down from information overload.

Example 2: Bar, Restaurant, and Music Venue

On a bar and restaurant website, the biggest problems found on the Accessibility tab had to do with navigation and wayfinding and timing and preservation. Another issue, not related to accessibility, was promoted to be a top 3 issue because of its impact on marketing. Let's take a look at the accessibility issues first:

Navigation and Wayfinding:

- UI elements do not have a visible focus indicator when targeted via keyboard navigation
- Pages are rarely separated into sections with appropriate headings
- A "skip link" is not provided at the top of any page
- Navigation includes nested pages that are also in the top-level navigation
- The user has no indication of where they are on the website
  Timing and Preservation:
- Users do not have sufficient time to complete ticket checkout
- Users are not provided with a mechanism to ask for a time extension during ticket checkout

This bar and restaurant is also a venue for music events and sells tickets. When users attempt to purchase tickets for an event, their session timer is set for a mere eight minutes. For users with motor impairments and cognitive disabilities, this limited time can exacerbate anxiety and cause the user to make mistakes during the checkout process. We might present the top 3 opportunities for improvement to the stakeholders like so:

1. Improve the ticket checkout experience. Increase the timer for checking out to 15 minutes to reduce errors during the process as well as decrease anxiety for users with cognitive impairments.

2. Refine the navigation. Remove redundant links. Streamline options by adding logical navigation groupings for event tickets, food and drink options, and updates. Add indicators for the user to know where they are on the website.

3. Implement modern email opt-in. The current newsletter form refuses new input, indicating to the user that the list is full. Implementing a more modern email list management tool will increase user trust and make managing updates easier.

Additional suggestions for website improvement support these three opportunities:

- Implementing a cookie policy and consent notification (made possible by moving to a new email newsletter provider)
- Adding a terms and conditions page to protect the owners of the website and define user behavior expectations
- Adding an accessibility statement that includes accessibility details for the physical location of the venue as well as the website

As you see, none of these issues is a "big deal" alone, but together they enhance the usability and accessibility of the website, making the user experience more positive and welcoming.

Example 3: Non-Profit Website

On a non-profit website, the primary accessibility issues found had to do with visual and auditory alternatives and navigation and wayfinding. Let's take a look at the issues identified with these accessibility features:

Visual and Auditory Alternatives:
- Some images on the website have text embedded in them
- No images on the website have alt text
- None of the complex images are given extended descriptions
- Information in complex images such as infographics is not also provided in the body text of the website
- Some color choices in complex infographics do not pass the color contrast minimum requirements

Navigation and Wayfinding:
- Pages do not have meaningful titles or headings
- Some pages on the website are not accessible from the menu

- No search function is available
- The heading hierarchy skips levels in many places

Additional accessibility issues were found in the content clarity and readability section but were deprioritized because another issue was promoted to be a top 3 issue: fundraising. Typically, there are only two ways a website visitor can support a non-profit: either by donating money or volunteering.

On this non-profit's website there is only one donation CTA, found in the primary navigation menu. A second way to donate is through an embedded widget provided by a third-party fundraising service. The primary CTA takes the user to a new page, then the user must scroll to find another button that opens the donation transaction process that is built into the website hosting. This is a complex process and gives the user many opportunities to get distracted and not complete the task of making a donation.

With all of this in mind, we might make these top 3 suggestions to our non-profit website stakeholders:

1. Prioritize donations. Increase the size of the button and text in the navigation. Make that same button the CTA through the website. Make sure clicking the button takes the user immediately to the donation page without additional page loads.

2. Make important information searchable in text. One of the primary images on the website has four important statistics embedded in the image. The statistics are not provided anywhere else on the website. Information found in complex infographics should also be found in website content. All important information should be available as body text, which improves the website's appearance in search engine results. All images on the website should have meaningful text alternatives.

3. Reduce information complexity. Add meaningful headings and page titles. Break up long passages into short, easy-to-read sections with appropriate headings and information hierarchy. Provide access to all pages of the website by adding a site map to the footer.

These three examples should explain how to communicate effectively with the stakeholders about the biggest problems on the website. All of the additional findings can be addressed in the future. Keep it simple. All you need to share is the minimum amount of information that will demonstrate your expertise and show that you've found issues that leave the website vulnerable to digital accessibility lawsuits and that you're the right person to fix them.

CREATE RECOMMENDATION VISUALS

Finally, before you bring your findings to stakeholders, you'll want to create a visual to describe the fix you're suggesting. Remember: Keep It Super Simple. You're not required or expected to do the work before you've been hired. To that end, keep your efforts to demonstrate your suggestions to the lowest fidelity possible.

Communicate your ideas using whatever method is easiest for you and is the most helpful to get the point across. This will, again, vary by issue found and by type of website. Here are the methods suggested, in order of effort, with the lowest effort first.

Screenshots with Annotations

This is an ideal way to demonstrate your knowledge and experience without doing any design work. Take a screenshot of the issue, draw lines with contrasting colors, and make brief but meaningful annotations about what should be done.

Example: Drawing a brightly colored box around the donate button in the top-level navigation for the non-profit and adding the note Make this bigger, with larger text. Make it easy for patrons to support your organization financially; you are asking for donations that will help change people's lives.

FIGURE 5.1 Image of a mock nonprofit website screenshot with a bright pink rectangle highlighting the light gray Donate button. A bright pink line connects the rectangle surrounding the button to the annotation which says: "The color of the primary call to action (CTA) button should be bright and vibrant–the loudest message to the person visiting the website that this is the action you want them to take."

"Franken-Mockups"

Franken-mockup is a term for "making a visual by mashing up screen-shots together until they're aligned with the way the website should look." It's exactly what it sounds like. Take a screenshot of a page. Then cover up parts of the screenshot with squares of color to blend in with the background or move buttons around by screenshotting just the button and changing its location. The end result is a stack of layers in a design tool that looks reasonably close to the end result of making changes in the code.

Example: There's a page on the beauty website where a video is embedded in the center of the screen, with centered text below it and a button further down. For the franken-mockup, we would take a screen-shot of the whole screen and cover up the content with a block the same color as the website background. Then, we would take a screenshot of the video placeholder image, shrink it a little, and move it to the right side of the screen. The text should be left-aligned and moved to the left of the video. The button then gets moved to below the text on the left side. All of these visual changes are done by taking screenshots of the parts and rearranging them on the screen.

Before

Video takes up too much space in the middle of the page, crowding the call to action suggesting the user make an appointment.

By shifting around some elements we can make some visual 'breathing room' for the important information.

FIGURE 5.2 Image of a slide showing the "before" screenshot of a website on the right side and text on the left. The header says "Before" and the text below it says "Video takes up too much space in the middle of the page, crowding the call to action suggesting the user make an appointment. By shifting around some elements we can make some visual 'breathing room' for the important information.

FIGURE 5.3 shows a slide from the same deck with all of the content from the screenshot cut out into individual pieces, scattered across the page. The text says "In Between"

After

We move the video to the right side of the screen where users can choose to engage if they want to.

Changing the location of "Ready to make an appointment" and the associated buttons makes it more clear what the user is expected to do.

FIGURE 5.4 shows a slide with the header "After" with the elements on the page rearranged in a pleasing way. The text is aligned along the left side, with the video on the right side of the page, about half the size it was previously. The buttons are now left-aligned and more closely associated with the text. The slide content says "We move the video to the right side of the screen where users can choose to engage if they want to. Changing the location of 'Ready to make an appointment" and the associated buttons makes it more clear what the user is expected to do.

Wireframes

Sometimes suggestions require taking away as many of the visual details as possible. If your suggestions include restructuring some of the parts of the website, you might find a simple wireframe is easiest to communicate the structural changes without allowing the stakeholders to get distracted by the existing content and visuals.

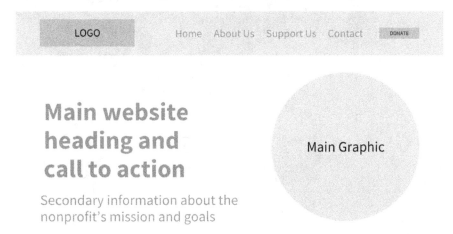

FIGURE 5.5 Screenshot of a gray-scale wireframe showing the approximate locations of content, without using specific sizes, parameters or content.

High-Fidelity Mockups and Prototypes

These are the most complex and time-consuming visuals to make, so avoid them whenever possible. These should be reserved for major design revamps, such as a scenario where your suggestion is to change the full color scheme and style of the website. They might also be useful in scenarios where you've already convinced the stakeholders to pay you to do a redesign, but they want to see your vision before agreeing to all changes. It is not necessary to use the same level of fidelity for all of the issues you've found, so use the lowest fidelity method that works for each issue.

In the following screenshot, the high-fidelity mockup is highly detailed, with rich colors, vibrant pictures, and realistic placeholder text.

FIGURE 5.6 High fidelity mockup of the imagined Memento Hotel website in full color.

In the next chapter, we'll bring our visuals and suggestions together into a nice-looking slide deck and then prepare for a presentation with stakeholders. We'll discuss how to effectively present the evaluation findings, our suggestions for improvement, and the next steps. You'll also learn how to confidently ask for stakeholder buy-in to do the redesign work.

CHAPTER 6

REPORT AND PRESENT

I n Chapter 4, you reviewed a website and found a number of accessibility and usability issues. You may have found just a handful of issues, or you may have identified several hundred small problems. Everything that you have discovered should be documented on the Website Accessibility and Usability Evaluation spreadsheet. In the previous chapter, you identified the most important accessibility and usability problems that should be brought to your stakeholders' attention.

Now your job is to report on those issues by creating a presentation for your stakeholders. In this chapter, you will learn how to select and describe the top 3 issues you discovered in a way that makes the stakeholders feel a sense of urgency to fix them. Developing the best way to do this is a skill that comes with practice, so do not feel like you need to be perfect at this the first time you do it. The best way to communicate these top 3 issues is with a slide deck.

USE A SLIDE DECK TEMPLATE

In the files you are granted access to as part of the purchase of this book, you will find a PowerPoint document (.pptx) titled [Template] Website Accessibility and Usability Evaluation Results Slide Deck. Download this blank template. Anytime you need to create a new slide deck, make a copy of this template to start fresh. Alternatively, you can use any slide deck template you prefer. Stick to a clear, simple slide deck template that is easy for non-technical stakeholders to understand. For this presentation, visual consistency and minimalism are more important than personality and decorative elements.

Below is an overview of the slides included in this slide deck:

FIGURE 6.1 Screenshot showing all 14 of the slides in the template

This slide deck has just 14 slides, but you may find it helpful to add more or remove some that are unnecessary.

UPDATE THE TEMPLATE

Slide 1

The deck starts with a slide showing the company name, which you will update to reflect the name of the company whose website you have reviewed. Be sure to update the byline with your own name. Change the image on this slide to the company logo, making sure to tweak the placement of the image so that it looks good. Reduce the size of the logo if it becomes blurry or difficult to read.

FIGURE 6.2 Screenshot of Slide 1

Slide 2

The second slide in the deck is a simple contents page, which describes what the stakeholders are going to find out from your presentation. There are just three things on this table of contents: Overview, Opportunities, and Recommendations. These are the sections of this slide deck and presentation: an overview of the process used to evaluate the website, the opportunities for improvement found, and the recommendations you make for improvement. You can add to this slide an image from the website, which can add some personalization to the delivery of your findings and help the stakeholders emotionally connect to the presentation. If needed, update this page with any additional content you have added.

FIGURE 6.3 Screenshot of Slide 2

Slide 3

Slide 3 is a transition slide, meant to give you the opportunity to set the context for the next section. Later in this chapter, we will review specific phrases you can use for impact, but for now, we will focus on the content of the slides. You shouldn't need to make any changes to this slide other than changing the background color or adding an image if it is appropriate.

Overview

FIGURE 6.4 Screenshot of Slide 3

Slide 4

On Slide 4, you will find bullet points that describe what the evaluation is assessing on the website. You can update these descriptions if needed.

Website Analysis

I assessed the existing website for these factors and made recommendations:

- **Accessibility** - Can users of all ability levels access the website?
- **Usability** - Can new users easily understand the website?
- **Information Architecture** - Is the website easy to navigate?
- **Visual Design** - Is the website aesthetically pleasing?
- **Content** - Is the website content clear and understandable?

FIGURE 6.5 Screenshot of Slide 4

Slide 5

Slide 5 is where you will add a general overview statement. If there is a discernible theme to the findings or a general statement that describes what you have discovered, this is an appropriate place to put it. It might be helpful to try to tie the findings to the theme of the website. For example, if presenting to a group of stakeholders for a medical spa website you reviewed, a statement might be: The MedSpa website is a good candidate for a lightweight face-lift. It is in need of just a little enhancement. Like a deft touch with a microblading scalpel, a steady hand and an eye for beautiful balance will do wonders. This statement is intended to put the stakeholders at ease, showing that you understand their business and have crafted the presentation accordingly.

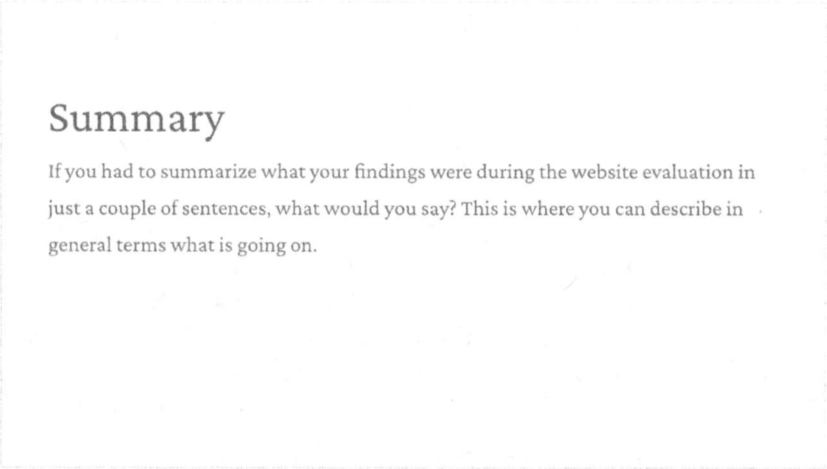

Summary

If you had to summarize what your findings were during the website evaluation in just a couple of sentences, what would you say? This is where you can describe in general terms what is going on.

FIGURE 6.6 Screenshot of Slide 5

Slide 6

The next slide, Slide 6, is another transition slide. Once you have introduced yourself and the overview of the presentation, it is time to dive into what you found through the evaluation of the website. We refer to issues as "opportunities" because that's what they are. Currently, these issues are causing friction in the user experience. They are each an opportunity to improve the experience and include users of all abilities. Once fixed, these are opportunities to re-engage the user and guide them toward revenue-driving activities.

FIGURE 6.7 Screenshot of Slide 6

DESCRIBE THE MOST IMPORTANT ISSUES

It is important to keep the stakeholders engaged through the presentation, which is why all of the previous slides have been "setting the mood" for the client. In the next slides, we will share our discoveries, the realization of which may bring discomfort to the stakeholders. Your job will be to describe the most important issues found and why they matter for accessibility and the customer's user experience.

Remember that stakeholders are real people, and many of them are disappointed when they find out that their website has not been a welcoming experience for users with disabilities. No business owner wants to alienate potential customers, and this next section has the potential to feel like a personal affront to them. Essentially, we are letting them know that they have done something objectively "wrong" regardless of their good intentions. Ensure you are delivering the details on these next few slides with compassion and the positive expectation that they will want to improve the experience for customers.

Slide 7

On slide 7, we want to narrow down our opportunities to just three things that the stakeholders should know about and fix on their website. Any more items than just three opportunities to focus on at first becomes quickly overwhelming. This is where we need to keep Miller's

Law in mind. As a reminder, Miller's Law is a psychological principle that states that the human brain can only process limited amounts of information at once, usually around seven pieces. Too much information feels overwhelming and causes people to "shut down" or become unable to make decisions. If we overwhelm our stakeholders with too much information, they will typically default to saying "no" or taking no action.

Whenever possible, combine opportunities into something a little bit larger or more general, which makes it easier to cover more detail in fewer opportunities. For instance, if there are multiple instances where the heading, body text, and link text all have color contrast issues, we might just say one opportunity is to address color contrast issues across the website. This is where you will take a bit longer to talk through the impact these issues have on the user experience and how they frustrate users with disabilities.

FIGURE 6.8 Screenshot of Slide 7

Slide 8

Slide 8 is an optional slide where, if needed, you can bring up small options for improvement. This could be an opportunity to suggest removing underlines from headings that are not linked to any other pages. This is a usability issue, but it can have a huge impact on users with regard to information architecture. Make sure that these opportunities are small and discrete, and are not as complex as the top 3 opportunities on the previous page.

FIGURE 6.9 Screenshot of Slide 8

SHOW YOUR IDEAS FOR IMPROVEMENT

Slide 9

Slide 9 is another transition slide where you can reassure the stakeholders that these issues are, indeed, fixable and introduce your plan to address them. You can add the company brand color to the background of this slide if you like. Make sure the headline maintains good color contrast.

Recommendations

FIGURE 6.10 Screenshot of Slide 9

Slide 10

The next slide, slide 10, is the place to briefly describe a suggested fix for each of the top 3 opportunities. You can speak to these issues in greater detail, but the text on this page should be short and succinct. The next three slides have room to go into more detail.

FIGURE 6.11 Screenshot of Slide 10

Slides 11–13

If the stakeholders seemed to feel negative about the previous section, over the next few slides you will have the chance to bring their energy back up again. Our goal here is to demonstrate that we are the right people to solve these problems. Slides 11 through 13 are where you will demonstrate your understanding of UX design and accessibility by showing your ideas for how to fix those issues.

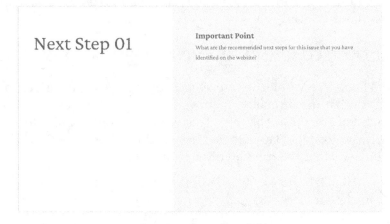

FIGURE 6.12 Screenshot of Slide 11

Remember the KISS method: Keep It Super Simple. Try to keep your suggestions as simple as possible. Your goal is to show the stakeholders what is possible and give them a taste of the work you can do. Here are a few examples.

The client is a non-profit organization seeking more donations and volunteers. Perhaps one of the issues you found on the website is that the donation button is very small or placed in a location that users are unlikely to notice. In this case, your visual might be a screenshot with a large red circle around the misplaced button. You can speak to how you would increase the size and prominence of the button to ensure users notice it. You might also create a visual showing where you suggest the button be placed and what size and color it should be.

In another example, the client is a music venue and you discovered through the website evaluation that the newsletter signup form has low color contrast. Visitors to the website think the form is broken and do not enter their information for updates. Your visual might be a screenshot of the issue, alongside a screenshot of changes you made in the browser.

For an HVAC client with a flashing video that automatically plays when the page loads, you might grab a GIF of the page and show it alongside a screenshot of the page with a vibrant but static header image. You can explain how the video flashing might be unpleasant for some users with cognitive impairments and describe how the static image communicates their brand better.

All of these examples are from actual projects completed by people who have followed this process and positively impacted the accessibility and usability of their clients' websites. These and other examples can be found in the Patreon community *https://www.patreon.com/maigenUX* at the free level.

CALL OUT LEGAL AND FINANCIAL IMPLICATIONS

Whenever possible, tie your suggestions to a positive business outcome. Describe the estimated improvement to the business if it chooses to implement these changes. This is also an opportunity to talk about any accessibility lawsuits that have impacted other companies in their industry that you can find through an online search.

Highlight how an inaccessible website can expose their business to unnecessary legal risk and mention that accessibility lawsuits are on the rise. (13)

If you have knowledge of the financial impact, consider describing how accessibility and usability issues directly affect the company's financial performance with regard to lost conversions, poor customer retention, or decreased site traffic.

If you can find relevant information through an online search, point out how improving usability and accessibility by implementing your recommendations can provide a return on investment (ROI). This can be an increase in conversion rates, improved user satisfaction, fewer service calls, and possibly an increase in new business.

Slide 14

The final slide of the deck, slide 14, is where you will finish the presentation by pitching your services to make the necessary changes on the client's website. Add your contact information and a note of appreciation.

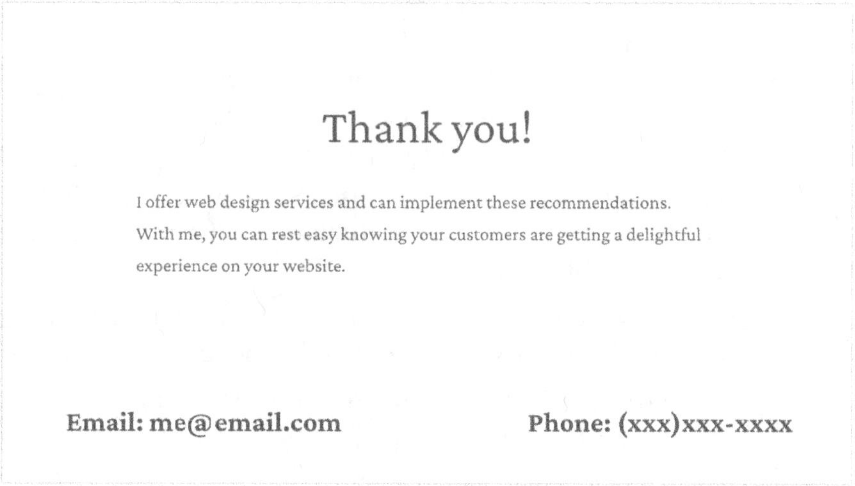

Thank you!

I offer web design services and can implement these recommendations. With me, you can rest easy knowing your customers are getting a delightful experience on your website.

Email: me@email.com   **Phone: (xxx)xxx-xxxx**

FIGURE 6.13 Screenshot of Slide 14

SCHEDULE A MEETING WITH STAKEHOLDERS

Once you have prepared the slide deck, reach out to the stakeholders to set up a 30-minute meeting. This can take place in person or over a video call.

To set this up, you will need to email or call the primary stakeholder and work together to decide on an appropriate time and location. Make sure all decision-making stakeholders will be able to attend this meeting. While on this phone call, get all email addresses of all attending stakeholders.

Follow Proper Meeting Etiquette

After this date and time have been finalized, follow proper meeting etiquette by sending a calendar invite. Here are the steps to follow to do this effectively:

1. Create a new event in your calendar software.

2. Give it an appropriate and meaningful event name, such as Website Evaluation Results for Wilson's Martini Bar. It should be unambiguous; the stakeholders should know exactly what meeting they are attending.

3. Get a link from your video meeting provider of choice. If you are using Google Calendar, you will be able to use Google Meet conferencing for free.

4. Add the meeting link to your calendar invite.

5. Add a brief agenda to the description of the meeting. This should be similar to the contents page of the slide deck and can look like this: In this meeting, we will discuss the process I used to evaluate the website, major opportunities for improvement, and my recommendations.

6. Check the details, such as the date and time, and that the agenda and meeting link have been entered correctly.

7. Add the email addresses of the stakeholders who you want to invite to the meeting.

8. Send the meeting invitation.

Ideally, the stakeholders will respond by accepting the meeting invite, though some small business owners do not use their calendars as effectively as others, so this might not happen. If they do not accept the meeting invite, make sure to follow up with them via phone call or email the day before to confirm attendance. If you send an email, you can include the meeting link in case they did not see the calendar invite.

Respect Everyone's Time

Be mindful of the time granted by scheduling a meeting that is long enough to cover everything but not so long that people will lose focus. For this meeting, 30 minutes is usually enough to review the slide deck and answer any stakeholder questions. This meeting is to demonstrate that you have the knowledge and expertise to help them address the issues you have found in a reasonable time frame.

You will want to manage your presentation pacing effectively by paying attention to the reactions and responses of the stakeholders. Move through your presentation at a steady pace, pausing to check for understanding and to answer any questions. As you transition between sections, ask "Does anyone have any questions?" and pause for at least 10 seconds to allow them to think before responding.

Be attuned to the level of engagement in the meeting by looking for nonverbal cues and body language. If stakeholders seem overwhelmed, bored, or confused, be ready to simplify your explanations or focus more on the points they are interested in. Making adjustments to your presentation on the fly is very normal and is one of the main reasons why effectively preparing for the presentation is so important. Ensure you are presenting at your best level by practicing your delivery at least three times.

Wrap It Up

Be prepared to answer any questions about your evaluation findings, recommendations, or next steps. If there are questions you can't answer immediately, make a note and follow up.

Always thank the stakeholders for their time and ask for feedback on the presentation and your recommendations. This is also the appropriate time to pitch your ability to do the work. Present yourself as the ideal candidate to implement these changes. Offer specific tasks you can handle post-evaluation, such as a full website redesign or accessibility fixes. The final page of the slide deck, the one with your contact information and note of thanks, should be visible on the screen during questions and final thank-yous.

Be honest about areas outside your expertise and recommend when they may need to hire a developer or specialist for particular tasks. For each recommended fix, be clear about what it will take to implement it (time, resources, and potential costs) and what steps should be prioritized.

Follow Up

After the meeting, send a follow-up email summarizing the discussion and set a clear deadline for responses or commitments to the next steps.

Reiterate that you have the ability to do the work. Explain why immediate action is essential, especially for critical issues such as accessibility or security vulnerabilities.

In the next chapter, we will talk about how to upsell your services to fix the issues you have presented.

CHAPTER 7

SELL YOURSELF TO DO THE WORK

You have evaluated the website. You have presented your findings. You have informed the stakeholders about accessibility, made them aware of the issues on their website and captured their interest. Now comes the part that makes many designers feel their stress levels rising: selling yourself to do the work.

Here is the good news: you have already done the hardest part. You have demonstrated your knowledge and expertise by finding real problems, documenting them, and suggesting practical solutions. Now all you need to do is make it official and get paid for putting your skills to work. Let's break this down into manageable steps.

PITCHING YOUR SERVICES

It is time to talk about money–specifically, your money. One of the biggest mistakes I see people make is severely undercharging for their services. Here is my strongest advice, up front: do not charge less than $50 per hour for your working time.

What to Charge

The topic of pricing makes many early-career designers uncomfortable. You might be tempted to charge $20-30 per hour just to get the work. Stop right there. Here's my firm rule: your minimum hourly rate should be $50, and you should be aiming for $75-100 per hour as an early-career designer focused on accessibility.

I know what you are thinking: "But I am just starting out!" It is important for you to know that you are worth at least $50 per hour. You have already invested time and money into your education. You understand accessibility and usability in ways that most small business owners do not. You are not just pushing pixels around, you are helping businesses avoid costly lawsuits and reach more customers.

It might be helpful to know that mid-career and senior designers typically charge $100 to $150 per hour, and that does not include accessibility expertise. Accessibility expertise is rare and valuable, and you can help save companies significant money in lawsuits and costly future remediation. Also remember that these rates do not include the same benefits as a salaried designer. Keep all of this in mind as you enter a conversation about money.

If that feels scary to ask for, keep in mind that these are very fair rates for skilled knowledge work. You made this career change to do more than just survive. Your rates will need to cover your basic living expenses, health insurance, retirement savings, professional development, taxes and, whenever possible, money to do something fun.

You are delivering real value. Price accordingly.

Having the Money Conversation

Before you start that money conversation, consider what work needs to be done. Then, create a couple of options for stakeholders to choose from. Everyone feels more empowered when they have choices, so it would be considered a best practice to give stakeholders a feeling of control: they are going to hire you and pay you to complete the work; options give them a chance to have a say in what the maximum expense will be. Here are a few basic package ideas you can use to base yours on:

Basic Package - $750

- 10 hours of remediation work, focusing on most critical accessibility issues.
- Includes basic documentation and handoff meeting
- One round of revisions included

Standard Package - $1500

- 20 hours of remediation work, remediating comprehensive accessibility issues

- Includes detailed documentation and handoff meeting
- Two rounds of revisions are included

Premium Package - $3000

- 35 hours of remediation work, focusing on a complete accessibility overhaul
- Includes extensive documentation of fixes made and the WCAG criterion the fixes addressed
- Unlimited revisions within the scope of the accessibility issues found
- Comprehensive handoff, including 30-day support period

These are just a suggestion, a place to start from when creating your proposal. Make adjustments to these prices and what is included to suit your level of ability.

Remember: never start the work without a deposit. It is typical to ask for 50% of the total as a deposit before the work begins, a payment of 25% at the midpoint (or when certain goals have been met) and 25% once the work has been completed. If you are proposing a set number of hours of work, you should require payment for the first 5 to 10 hours spent.

Some small business owners may have never worked with a designer or accessibility specialist and feel unsure of how to work together. They may ask for just a few hours of work to see how things go. This is a good opportunity for both parties to learn more about each other's working style and build a relationship. This is not a bad thing, and you will always learn something about working with clients.

What to Say When Offering Your Services

If you have not offered your services and asked for compensation before, it probably feels intimidating to start the conversation. Keep in mind, when discussing rates with potential clients, confidence is key. You are not asking for permission to charge these rates - you are stating your professional fees.

Here is a basic script for discussing your rates:

"Based on the issues we identified in the evaluation, I estimate this will take about [X] hours at $50 per hour. I typically require a 50% deposit to begin work, which would be [amount]. Would you like me to put together a formal proposal?"

Keep it simple, and remember to finish your sentences with a period and then stop talking. Let the stakeholder respond, even if they leave silence hanging in the air for a few seconds. Those seconds will feel like minutes, but this is an investment in their business and they deserve an opportunity to consider it.

If they balk at the rate, you could say: "I understand budget concerns. However, considering that a single accessibility lawsuit typically costs $25,000 or more, investing in proper remediation now is actually quite cost-effective. We could also break this into phases to spread out the investment."

This is your opportunity to create and describe your plan for how you will prioritize the highest impact issues to address first. You DO have the ability and knowledge to help them, ability and knowledge they do not have themselves. You CAN do this work.

Understanding Proposals vs. Statements of Work (SOWs)

Before we dive into estimating work and structuring proposals, let's clarify the difference between a Proposal and a Statement of Work (SOW):

- A proposal is a pitch that outlines what you can do for a client, why they should hire you, and how much it will cost. It's usually sent before a contract is signed and can be more flexible.
- A Statement of Work (SOW) is a binding agreement that outlines the specific deliverables, timeline, and scope of the project. It's more detailed than a proposal and helps prevent scope creep.

Think of it this way: A proposal is like a menu; it presents options and pricing. A Statement of Work is more like a recipe. It provides step-by-step details of what will be delivered.

What Goes Into a Website Design Refresh Proposal?

Here is a general structure for a strong website design refresh proposal:

1. Introduction – A warm, personalized greeting that shows you understand the business's needs.
2. Project Goals & Objectives – What this work is intended to accomplish. Keep it high-level but clear.

3. Deliverables & Scope of Work – List exactly what you'll provide, ensuring there's no ambiguity.

4. Timeline & Milestones – A rough breakdown of how long things will take.

5. Pricing & Payment Terms – Transparent breakdown of costs, including deposits.

6. Next Steps & Call to Action – Encourage them to ask questions, book a call, or move forward.

It is typical to use the proposal to sell the project and use the SOW to define the execution once the small business owners have agreed.

How to Estimate UX Work (Especially Small Fixes)

Estimating small accessibility fixes can be tricky, especially since you do not want to inadvertently undercharge but also need to keep pricing easy to say yes to for small businesses. It is ideal to start with time-based estimations, knowing that you will get better at this over time, as you complete the work.

Basic fixes might take 1-3 hours. Some of these tasks might include alt text updates, button contrast fixes, minor heading hierarchy adjustments.

Medium fixes might take 4-8 hours. These tasks can include fixing navigation issues, restructuring page layouts, implementing better form labels.

Complex fixes can take 10 hours or more. Some complex fixes might include redesigning major sections or pages, creating completely new content for multiple areas of the site, or documenting additional fixes to be done when time and budget allow.

Bundle quick fixes into flat-rate packages, like so:

- Accessibility Quick Fix ($750) is 10 hours of targeted remediation.
- Usability Upgrade ($1,500) is more like 20 hours of work, addressing broader usability issues.
- Full Website Audit & Fix ($3,000) which includes comprehensive UX and accessibility improvements.

Don't forget to factor in discovery time, or the time it takes to find all of the issues that need to be fixed. Even small fixes require time to test, document, and validate changes. Build in at least 1-2 hours of prep and post-testing into your estimates.

It is a good idea to use a three-option pricing model for two reasons: First, it is easier to create. Second, it is a familiar pattern for people. When you offer three pricing tiers, you can put the absolute bare minimum in the lowest-cost tier. Make the middle tier the most attractive for price plus value. Add all of the extensive fixes to the third tier and charge the highest rate. Buying psychology says that when consumers are presented with three pricing options, they often gravitate toward the middle choice. This behavior is influenced by several psychological principles:

Compromise Effect: Introduced by Itamar Simonson, this principle suggests that consumers avoid extremes and choose the middle option, perceiving it as a balanced and justifiable choice.

Decoy Effect: Adding a third, less attractive option can steer consumers toward a specific choice. For example, if a high-priced option is introduced, it can make the middle option appear more reasonable, increasing its selection rate.

Good-Better-Best Pricing: Also known as "Goldilocks pricing," this strategy offers products at multiple price points. Consumers often select the "better" (middle) option, perceiving it as a balance between cost and quality.

By understanding these principles, you can structure your pricing to guide consumers toward preferred options. Your middle option should be the one that gives you the most flexibility and pay while delivering fixes you are proud to show off in your portfolio.

Suggested Time For Fixing Accessibility Issues

The following is a table with 25 small-to-medium accessibility fixes along with estimated time to complete each one. This should give you a clear idea of what to expect when working on small business websites. Please know that these are simply estimates, and if you have not already done similar work you should estimate your time slightly higher.

Accessibility Fix	Estimated Time to Complete
Add alt text to images	10-15 min per image
Fix color contrast issues	30 min - 1 hr per page
Ensure proper heading hierarchy	1-2 hrs per website
Add descriptive link text	30 min - 1 hr per page
Label form fields properly	30 min - 1 hr per form
Ensure keyboard navigability	2-3 hrs per website
Fix missing or incorrect ARIA labels	1-2 hrs per website
Add closed captions to videos	1-3 hrs per video
Create and provide a transcript for audio content	30 min - 2 hrs per audio file
Ensure focus indicators are visible	1-2 hrs per website
Fix incorrect tab order	2-3 hrs per website
Ensure error messages are clear and accessible	1-2 hrs per form
Improve mobile accessibility	2-4 hrs per website
Ensure proper text spacing and line height	30 min - 1 hr per website
Add skip-to-content links	1-2 hrs per website
Test and fix keyboard traps	1-2 hrs per website
Remove auto-playing media or provide controls	1-2 hrs per media item
Fix modal/dialog focus management	2-4 hrs per website
Ensure forms provide helpful validation messages	2-3 hrs per form
Ensure all buttons and controls have accessible labels	1-2 hrs per website
Provide alternative text for infographics	30 min - 1 hr per infographic
Fix layout issues that disrupt reading order	2-3 hrs per website
Ensure consistent navigation structure	2-4 hrs per website
Improve readability with better typography	1-2 hrs per website
Conduct an accessibility test with a screen reader	2-4 hrs per website

These estimations are based on the level of effort required for each fix, keeping in mind early-career designers who may need extra time for research and troubleshooting. The times align with rough industry estimates for freelance web designers/developers working on accessibility fixes.

WebAIM and Deque University training materials often suggest that basic remediations can take anywhere from a few minutes to a couple of hours, while more complex fixes can take several hours to days depending on site structure.

Many of these fixes scale depending on the website size and complexity. For example: Alt text fixes for 10 images might take 1-2 hours, but if a site has 200 images, it could take a full day or more (especially if missing descriptions need to be written). Similarly, fixing forms depends on how many fields need labels or validation improvements.

Remember, even "quick" fixes require testing with assistive technologies like screen readers or keyboard navigation. Time estimates should include that validation step to ensure changes actually improve accessibility.

Be Honest (With Yourself) About Your Abilities

This is where impostor syndrome often presents itself. You might start feeling doubts about yourself and your abilities. Here is what you need to keep top of mind: you do not need to be an expert in everything to deliver value. There is no expectation from your potential customers for you to know everything.

What you are qualified to do:

- Testing and Documentation
  - Perform manual testing
  - Use automated testing tools
  - Identify accessibility issues
  - Create accessibility documentation
  - Create testing reports
  - Document requirements for developers
- Strategic Planning
  - Suggest usability improvements and alternative solutions

- Prioritize accessibility fixes
- Create remediation roadmaps
- Use annotations to make specific design recommendations
- Create visual mockups to show potential design changes
- Provide implementation guidelines
- Technical Implementation
  - Fix color contrast issues
  - Add proper alt text to images
  - Create video and audio transcription using online tools
  - Implement proper heading hierarchy
  - Update form labels and instructions
  - Adjust text spacing and size
  - Add ARIA labels where appropriate (and remove inappropriately applied ARIA labels)
  - Make basic HTML/CSS code modifications
  - Update website content in a Content Management System (CMS) like Wordpress, Wix, Squarespace, Joomla, etc.
  - Communicate with developers about changes

That list should make you feel empowered! You can do so many things that can impact the business' bottom line. Now do you see how you can definitely apply your skills and knowledge to make accessibility updates?

There are many things that are outside of your scope of responsibility, though. Here are a few suggestions for what you should pass to others:

- Complex JavaScript functionality (really fancy interaction design and animations)
- Backend development (writing code that handles server-side operations like user authentication or processing form submissions)
- Server configurations (setting up and managing web servers, SSL certificates, or domain settings)

- Database work (building, adding to, or managing large tables of complex data)
- Enterprise-level system integrations (making an application connect to an application built by other people)
- Custom widget development (creating new functionality for the website)

It is perfectly okay–and professional–to say "That's beyond my current expertise, but I can help you find someone who specializes in that area." You are not expected to know everything, nor should you. There will always be someone able to do what you cannot. If you are worried about what you should say in such cases, here's a brief script to get you started:

"That's a great question about [complex issue]. While that's beyond my current expertise, I can help you define the requirements and find a qualified developer to implement that specific feature. This ensures you get the best possible solution while I focus on the accessibility improvements I specialize in."

What is the Meaning of "Done"

Before you start any work, you and the stakeholder need to come to a crystal clear agreement on what "done" means. This is for your benefit as much as it is for theirs. For you, it helps ensure you do not take on more work than you agreed on and are paid to do. For the client, it ensures they understand the boundaries of what you will do for the agreed upon price.

Setting expectations for any project, regardless of the context, is important. To make sure that all parties have the same expectations, before you begin, you should create a specific, measurable list of deliverables that will signal project completion. This will be entirely dependent upon the website and the accessibility and usability issues found. For your first project, this could be as simple as a spreadsheet containing a list of all issues found, and the steps taken to remediate them in a column beside each issue. You could make it more complex and include before and after screenshots in a text document that also includes the steps taken to remediate all issues. Start with the simplest possible documentation, and increase complexity as you get feedback and experience.

YOUR LEGAL REQUIREMENTS

What about the practical side of getting paid? First, this is not legal advice. Your most important step in this chapter will be to find out what laws apply to you. However, when you are first starting out, you should keep it as simple as possible.

Business Entity or Independent Contractor

For your first few projects, working as an independent contractor is usually sufficient. The bare minimum requirements are to have a Social Security Number or a Tax ID. In the United States, if a business pays an individual more than $600 over the course of one calendar year, the business is required to have that individual fill out a W-9 form and send a 1099 document after the year closes, for tax purposes. This ensures that taxable income is recorded and taxed appropriately. An independent contractor would claim that income on their taxes, and it will be taxed at that individual's rate, which is dependent on other taxable income received from other entities through the year.

If, for example, you only charged your first client $500 for the work performed, there is no requirement to report that income federally. That business might have internal accounting rules that require them to send you a 1099 or fill out a W-9, regardless of the amount paid. If you are following this book to get real world experience for your portfolio and do not intend to freelance exclusively, you likely do not need to do anything else.

It is recommended that you set up a separate bank account to use for these contract projects, and keep records of all income and expenses. You should also set aside about 25-30% of this income to pay taxes, as contract labor is not usually taxed.

If your annual income from working with clients exceeds $30,000, that might be an indication you should set up a business entity such as an LLC (Limited Liability Company) or a corporation. Remember, this isn't legal or tax advice. Consider consulting a tax professional or a lawyer for specific guidance.

How to Get Paid

When you are first starting out and testing the waters with freelancing, do not overthink the details and just get paid as easily as possible. You can use any method that your customer feels comfortable with. Old fashioned modes like cash and check work perfectly. Digital payment platforms like Venmo, Paypal, CashApp and Zelle make it easy to send money. You might also set up a business bank account and connect it to a Stripe account, which will allow you to send basic and professional invoices. You could acquire a Square card reader and the app and take instant payments on your phone.

Digital payment platforms provide payment records and often offer basic invoicing. They handle payment processing and work with most accounting software. Not to mention, they are widely trusted with hundreds of thousands of daily transactions.

Pro Tip: Create separate business accounts on these platforms. Do not mix personal and business transactions. Your future self (and accountant) will thank you.

Check Local Requirements

You might consider checking the local requirements before starting to do professional services work like this. Some locations may require business licenses for certain kinds of work. It is unlikely, but you might have different tax obligations or insurance requirements. It depends on your location, as some cities require licenses for even home-based or online businesses. Check your local Small Business Development Center (SBDC) or local government website.

When in doubt, consult local small business resources or a tax professional. Remember, starting simple is okay. You can always upgrade your business structure as you grow and take on more clients and larger projects.

GETTING STARTED ON THE WORK TO BE DONE

In this final section, we will talk about how to define, document and deliver your professional work. Often, early-career designers skip a very important step on the path to delivering a successfully completed project: clearly explaining the work to be done. Most of the time, they do this because they do not know any better. You, however, are going to be up for success from the beginning by creating a clear statement of work.

Creating an SOW (Statement of Work)

A Statement of Work (SOW) is your project's roadmap. It protects both you and your client by clearly defining the scope of the work that has been agreed to. Think of it as your "here is the plan of exactly what we are doing" document. Having an SOW will save you many headaches down the road.

Here is what needs to go into your SOW:

- Project Overview: Start with a brief summary of what you're going to do. Keep it simple - something like: "This project will address critical accessibility issues on [Business Name]'s website, focusing on WCAG 2.1 Level AA compliance for the home page and contact forms."

- Specific Deliverables: List exactly what you're going to provide, specifically. Instead of saying "fix accessibility issues," break it down like this:

  - Update color contrast on all buttons and text elements
  - Add proper alt text to 15 product images
  - Fix heading hierarchy on 5 key pages
  - Add proper form labels to the contact form
  - Provide documentation of all changes made
  - Deliver a final report showing before/after screenshots

- Timeline: Break down when things will happen. For example:
  - Week 1: Initial setup and color contrast fixes
  - Week 2: Image alt text and heading hierarchy updates
  - Week 3: Form accessibility improvements
  - Week 4: Testing and documentation
  - Week 5: Review and revisions

- Describe your working process: Explain how you'll actually do the work. For instance: "I will work on a development copy of the website to test changes before implementing them on the live site. Weekly progress updates will be provided via email, with screenshots of completed work."

- List what you need from stakeholders: Anything required from the client, including content, copy, or additional details, such as:
  - Access to their website backend
  - Brand guidelines (if they exist)

- Timely feedback (specify how quickly you need responses)
- Point of contact for questions
- Define what is NOT included. This is super important. Clearly state what is outside the scope of the project, like:
  - Content creation or rewriting
  - Design changes unrelated to accessibility
  - Performance optimization
  - Browser compatibility testing beyond current versions
  - Training for their team (unless specifically included)

Establish Communication Guidelines

Sometimes it feels awkward to be so detailed about everything. But clear communication will make your life so much easier. Here are some details you might think about including along with your SoW and ensuring that your client understands.

How often will you update the stakeholders? Once weekly is usually enough to ensure everyone knows how the project is moving along. What is the best way to reach you? Do you prefer email or text messages, or will the client invite you to share a Slack channel to communicate more easily with their team?

Make sure to let them know your regular working hours. You may not only work within these hours, but this will help establish and protect your professional boundaries. Stakeholders will understand that you do not pick up the phone after 6pm on weekdays. With these boundaries comes expectation setting: what is the response time they can expect from you? If they message at 11am on a Tuesday, when should they expect to hear from you with a response? Within 24-48 hours is industry-standard.

Document Everything

Keep a record of all decisions made, questions asked and answers given, feedback received, updates given, and time spent on tasks. All documentation should be kept in the same place, which might be in a shared Google Drive folder or other agreed-upon location.

After every conversation, take a few minutes before moving on to another task and send a quick email summary: "Confirming what we discussed…" This will save so many conversations later where one or both of you say something like "But I thought you said…"

Manage Scope Creep

It happens to literally every designer, and it will happen to you: the client will ask for "just one small thing" that was not part of the original plan. Here is a quick script for how to professionally handle the situation with grace: "I understand you'd like to add [new request]. That wasn't included in our original scope, but I'm happy to help! Would you like me to prepare a separate estimate for that work, or would you prefer to add it to our current project for an additional [X] hours at my standard rate?"

What is the Meaning of "Done" For Real?

We described defining "done" earlier in this chapter, which was essentially to make a list of the final criteria that both parties agree means the work on the project is complete. There are a few additional details that might be helpful. Here are the basic steps to wrap up a professional project of any size:

Schedule a Final Review Meeting with all stakeholders. This is your opportunity to demonstrate all of the fixes you have made and show the before-and-after comparisons. In this meeting, you will walk through all documentation and answer any questions from the team. This is also an appropriate time to share a clean, organized file that includes a summary of all implemented changes. You might include screenshots of key fixes for some of these changes. Clearly outline and point out any new processes the team should follow, such as alt text best practices, or guidance on future color choices. If you have documented any recommendations for future improvements, be sure to include those here as well.

Provide a final invoice at this meeting, or let the stakeholders know when to expect a digital invoice. This final invoice should contain a clear breakdown of work completed and any agreed-upon extras. It should also outline payment terms and your preferred payment method. Lastly, it should include a brief and sincere thank you note for trusting you with this important project. This meeting is usually the most positive and happy one you will experience in the whole project lifecycle, outside of the kickoff meeting. This is also a great time to ask them for a testimonial and feedback.

Remember, you are not just fixing accessibility issues. You are building relationships and establishing yourself as a processional. The way you handle documentation and communication is just as important as your technical skills.

By following these guidelines, you will come across as organized and professional, making it easy for clients to refer you to friends and colleagues with respect for your expertise.

CHAPTER 8

CREATE A CASE STUDY

In this final chapter of the book, we will discuss how to turn your website accessibility and usability evaluation presentation into a portfolio case study. By the end of this chapter, you will be able to explain the real or potential impact of the evaluated website on its users. You will also be able to update your portfolio with this case study and describe how you can make an impact on any organization as a freelance or in-house designer.

The most exciting news is that you have already done all of the heavy lifting required to make this a valuable addition to your portfolio. By using the template provided in Chapter 6 to create a stakeholder-focused presentation slide deck, you have significantly reduced the effort needed in this chapter. The presentation you have already created is your foundation. Unlike most of the case study formats we see today, it is already written with a focus on the end-user of a case study: a person looking to hire *you*, someone who can make a positive impact on their business. Whether they are a hiring manager, a recruiter, or a business owner, they want to know your work's real-world impact.

Most readers of your case study do not need—or want—to know every step you took between identifying the problem and delivering the outcome. Instead of starting with identifying the problem and painstakingly walking the reader through your process, we are going to lead with outcomes and impact. Why? Because that is what hiring managers and potential freelance clients care about the most.

DESCRIBE IMPACT

Which of these impact statements from a case study sounds more impressive?

- Impact Statement 1: "I conducted a website accessibility evaluation and found 47 issues"

- Impact Statement 2: "I identified ways to increase a service provider's market reach by making their website fully keyboard-navigable, opening their services to customers who can't use a mouse—including elderly users, who make up 35% of their target demographic"

The second one not only sounds impressive but is more specific.

One of these examples simply states a method the designer used and the immediate results of that activity. The other example describes the impact on the business as a result of conducting the website evaluation, without mentioning the method used or the steps taken to address the issues found during the evaluation. This kind of impact statement requires second-order thinking. You can use second-order thinking in every one of your case studies, so next we will define it and describe how to use it.

Using Second-Order Thinking

In his book The Most Important Thing: Uncommon Sense for the Thoughtful Investor, Oaktree Capital Management co-founder Howard Marks introduces second order of thinking. You may not have learned about second-order thinking yet, so here is a simple but relatable example. First-order thinking is like seeing that it is raining outside and grabbing an umbrella. It is the immediate, obvious solution to the immediate problem. Second-order thinking considers what happens next: "If I take my umbrella to work, I will need to find a place to put the wet umbrella in the office. It might drip on others in the elevator. Also, if I leave it at work by accident, I might not have it when I need it over the weekend."

Second-order thinking is about looking beyond the immediate solution to consider the ripple effects—not just "What happens next?" but "What happens after that, and after that?"

In UX, a first-order thought might be, "We should add a 'dark mode' option because users are asking for it!" Second-order thinking asks, "How will this affect our design system? Will we need to update all our images? How will we maintain consistency across both modes? What about third-party integrations?" Another example might be, "I want to add this cool animation to make the interface more engaging." Second-order thinking asks, "How will this affect loading time? What about users with motion sensitivity? Will this make the interface harder to understand or maintain?"

Thinking about the compound effects of a design decision is a skill learned over time, but the earlier you can learn it, the more successful your career will be. This is not a skill you will see defined in a job description, but your ability to demonstrate this in your case studies will help you stand out from your peers in any situation.

Focus on Business Value

By conducting the type of website evaluation you have learned from this book, you can provide tangible value to any business. Showing that in your case study simply requires thinking of the second-order consequences that will result from completing the fixes you recommended to stakeholders. To update the stakeholder slide deck and make it appropriate for your portfolio, you will need to make some small changes to the presentation. These changes will drive home the point for readers of the case study: that you are the person to hire who can make a difference for their business.

The people who are hiring you want to feel assured that you have some idea of how to connect what you do to an improved business outcome. To do this, you will need to consider numbers that matter. Look for opportunities to estimate:

- Increase in the number of users with improved access to the site
- Accessibility score improvements (such as going from 65 to 90 using the Lighthouse auditing tool)
- Reduction in the number of errors made by users
- Percentage of images with proper alt text
- Reduction in the time and/or effort required for customer support
- Increase in mobile usability
- Legal compliance standards are now met (and what meeting them prevents)
- Increase in user satisfaction
- Decrease in shopping cart abandonment rate
- Increase in time spent on site

All of these estimations can demonstrate what you bring to an organization, and you can determine these *without actually making the changes on a website*. Just by including them in the case study, you can show the impact you are capable of making. This is how to connect your work to business goals.

Because you have not yet fixed the accessibility issues you found in the website evaluation, these are estimates. Estimates are perfectly okay to include in case study summaries and can be tested once the changes have been made.

IMPORTANT: Most early-career designers are not aware of the rate at which design work is abandoned, not used, or used but never makes it into the actual product. 70% of the work an in-house designer does is never seen by customers or does not make it into the version that is released. Remember: Design is the cheapest form of development.

Make Metrics Meaningful

Raw numbers are not enough—you need to give them context. Telling a story is the only way to help other humans understand why information matters. Numbers tell us what happened, but stories help us understand why it matters to real people. Here are two examples of ways you can make your information tell a story and communicate effectively with other people:

Before: "I found and fixed 47 accessibility issues on 12 pages of the website." This is not enough context for what impact these changes could have on the user experience. Are they changes to the login page (high impact) or to the FAQ page (low impact)? Do the changes impact a large number of users (navigation) or a small number of users (climate pledge page)? Ambiguous language forces the reader to make up the rest of the story.

After: "I optimized the websites navigation to meet WCAG 2.1 AA standards, enhancing the user experience for an estimated additional 50,000 potential users per month, including individuals who rely on screen readers or have vision-related disabilities. These changes could translate into a 15% increase in target market reach, improving inclusivity and expanding our customer base." This statement paints a clear picture for the reader and immediately shifts their mindset to considering what benefit you can bring to the company, not wondering about your skills.

We can consider another example next. Before: "Mobile usability improved by 25%." This is a brief and direct statement with a quantified impact. Consider, however, what detail there is for a hiring manager or potential future client to extract and apply to the situation they would hire you for. A 25% increase in mobile usability does not inform the reader about the kind of usability issues that were addressed and to what degree of improvement. It also does not include detail that is more valuable to the context they need: how did the improvement of mobile usability increase revenue?

After: "By fixing accessibility issues and implementing responsive design best practices, we estimate mobile cart completion rates can be improved from 45% to 60%, potentially resulting in an additional 50 successful mobile purchases per month as well as an increase in total cart value." Those are the details that can make you stand out from all other applicants for any role.

SHOW OUTCOMES OVER OUTPUT

Showing outcomes over output means showing the result of the work you did, not the work itself. "Show your work" is for math class, not mobile apps. The reason you are worth the salaries paid to UX designers is that you bring the business more money than it spends to employ you. Your boss and your boss's boss do not care how you got the work done; they want to know that you did the work and you did it in a way that benefits them. Show outcomes.

These impact statements that speculate on the improvements to a business in terms of increased revenue or decreased costs should be displayed in close proximity to the visual demonstration of the changes to be made. Whenever possible, show the changes in context. If your improvement to the navigation involves color contrast updates, create the mockup to align with the visual changes. If your suggestions include information architecture or structural changes, create a sitemap to visualize the changes. If you suggest creating a new section of the website for articles, mock up what that new section would look like. The following figure, Figure 8.1, shows an example of an outcome in the form of an annotated screen:

FIGURE 8.1 Screenshot of a slide with annotations suggesting specific fixes for focus indicators

Not every suggested change will have an accompanying visual, but humans are visual creatures. Try to have at least two visuals in each case study. Focus visuals on anything that can show accessibility improvements, usability enhancements, problem resolutions, and risk reduction. Basically, show off the ways you can make the business more money or help it save money.

In the following two figures, Figure 8.2 and Figure 8.3, you can see that the problem and the solution have been detailed in annotations.

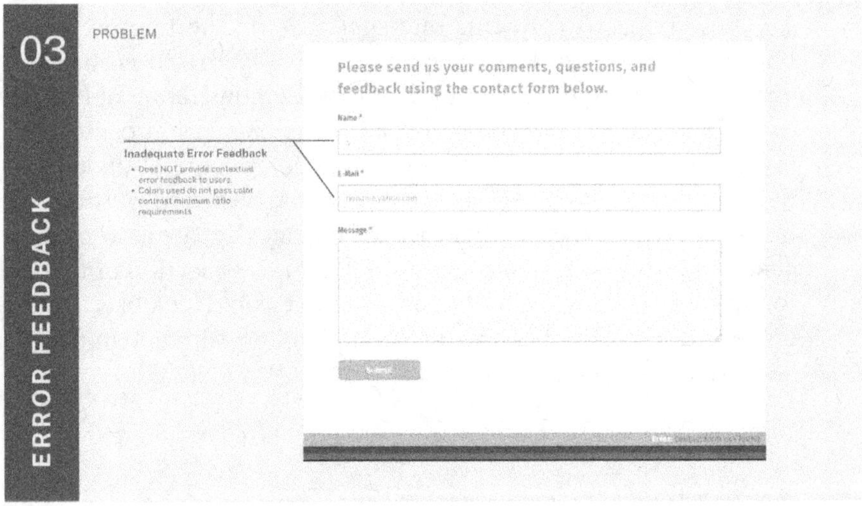

FIGURE 8.2 Screenshot of a slide with annotations showing inadequate error feedback for a form

FIGURE 8.3 Screenshot of a slide with annotations showing suggestions for improving error feedback on a form

Use a Template for Showing Outcomes

Let's take a look at a template you can use to create and iterate your impact or outcome statement: "Through [specific action], I expect [business type] to achieve [estimated result], leading to [business impact]." It takes practice to get better at creating these statements for maximum impact and you are not expected to be a talented marketing copywriter to achieve success. To that end, try using this template with your favorite AI tool.

Supply the tool with a general idea of the size of the audience and the basic data surrounding general disabilities, along with the impact statement, and ask it to create a few examples of how you can describe the potential impact of the accessibility improvements you suggested. You are guaranteed to get at least one idea that sparks your creativity, and you will get the hang of creating these statements over time. Always edit the output of an AI tool in your own words. Remember, you should be able to explain what the impact statement means in plain language. The level of formality of an impact statement in your case study should "speak the same language" as the hiring managers, clients, and recruiters reading it. Stay away from overly formal language and technical jargon.

The following is another brief template for showing outcomes:

1. Challenge: [One-sentence context about the issue, why it impacts users with disabilities]

2. Solution: [One sentence about what you did]

3. Impact: [List at least one specific outcome]

Notice how simple the format is. Early-career designers should avoid the temptation to use overly complex language to describe their work. Using plain, clear language demonstrates the ability to speak to anyone on the team with clear communication skills.

MAKE THE MINIMUM VIABLE CASE STUDY

The industry is currently overwhelmed by what the UX Collective described in 2018 as "The Case Study Factory." (14) Most case studies created by early-career designers are geared toward one audience and presumed to work for all audiences. That could not be further from the truth. The typical format is long-form writing that goes into detail about every phase of the design process followed—most often the Design Thinking Process.

The Design Thinking process was popularized in the late 90s by IDEO (which they explicitly branded as "Design Thinking" in the 2000s). Design Thinking was further evangelized by Tim Brown, CEO of IDEO, in his influential 2009 book *Change by Design*, which explained Design Thinking to a broader business audience and helped position it as a critical tool for innovation in organizations. Furthermore, Tim Brown's 2009 TED Talk and other media appearances introduced Design Thinking to a global audience, making it synonymous with creativity and innovation.

In the mid-2010s, UX/UI bootcamps such as General Assembly, Flatiron School, and Springboard began teaching Design Thinking as a fundamental methodology for product design and development. Other bootcamps followed suit, and the style became the de facto format used by UX/UI designers around the world. Seeing this format of case study used by so many of their peers has led many early-career designers to believe they should also follow this format. It is easy to understand why, but following the example set by so many others is no way to stand out when applying for your next job. To truly differentiate yourself from the crowded candidate market, your case study should be significantly different. Leveraging the slide deck created as part of the *Practical UX* process is one way to do that.

You see, the *Practical UX* process focuses on delivering the most value with the least amount of work. From the perspective of the person hiring you, that is ideal. Typically, a freelancer charges an hourly rate. Demonstrating efficiency shows that you will not burden a client project with unnecessary tasks and activities to drive up your pay. Similarly, a hiring manager looking to bring on an in-house designer is looking for someone who will not be wasteful of company resources and can problem solve without excessive busywork. Your case study, created while following the outline in this book, is already a concise story. You may not have noticed while reading or conducting the activities, but the format follows a traditional storytelling structure: Challenge, Struggle, Transformation.

Take a look at your case study and notice how it quickly gets to the point by showcasing the challenge (accessibility issues) first, followed by the struggle (how these accessibility barriers impact users with disabilities) and the transformation (the suggested improvements). Without needing to write a single line of code, you have created a satisfying story that can be translated to any website and understood by any reader of the case study.

Notice that your new case study does not include the typical characteristics of an early-career designer or bootcamp graduate portfolio. There is no lengthy process documentation, in-depth research method explanation, or screenshots of multiple design iterations. Unnecessary technical specifications and project management details are not essential to tell the story of what you are capable of. Your future employer wants to know the business context, the problem, and the solution highlights. You have learned a process for making those details easier to discern and communicate.

Doing the work to remediate the accessibility issues is another case study entirely. If you are a freelance designer and want to take on that job, pitch your services as directed in the previous chapter. If you are looking for a role as an in-house designer, this case study is now complete and ready to add to your portfolio. Now that you understand the process, you can start on another website evaluation project to add another case study to your portfolio. Remember, this process can also be used to evaluate web applications as well and makes for a great first project in the first 90 days in a new job.

UPDATE YOUR PROFESSIONAL DETAILS

You have now completed a professional case study using highly compensated skills that are going to be increasingly desirable in the immediate future. Now is the time to update your professional details so you show up in searches for recruiters looking for skills like these.

Update Your Resume

The following are some ideas for points you can add to your resume. Try adding these under freelancing work or a section for projects:

- Assessed small business and non-profit websites following WCAG 2.2 to identify accessibility barriers that prevent customers from engaging with content and purchasing goods and services, and that often lead to digital accessibility lawsuits
- Prepared detailed presentation slide decks highlighting critical accessibility issues identified through expert heuristic evaluation
- Designed actionable solutions to address accessibility barriers in order to improve overall website usability
- Helped small businesses identify and resolve critical accessibility barriers
- Conducted comprehensive WCAG 2.2 evaluations
- Helped non-profit organizations avoid potential ADA compliance issues while improving user experience for all customers

Update Your LinkedIn Profile

You have done excellent work; now make sure you get credit for it by showcasing your impact effectively. Consider updating your LinkedIn headline with some version of these ideas:

- Accessibility-focused UX designer helping small businesses protect their income and expand their market through inclusive design
- Specialist in WCAG compliance and usability improvements
- UX designer specializing in accessibility and usability
- UX designer helping businesses avoid $25k+ in accessibility lawsuit risks

Some skills you might consider adding to your LinkedIn profile in the Skills section if they are not already present:

- Usability testing
- Accessibility auditing (WCAG 2.1/2.2)
- Website accessibility

- User research
- Heuristic evaluation
- Stakeholder communication
- Website evaluation and optimization
- Information architecture
- Wireframing and prototyping
- Responsive web design
- Design thinking
- Customer journey mapping
- Web analytics and optimization
- UI design
- Presentation skills
- Client relationship management
- Digital strategy consulting

Finally, Congratulations!

Congrats on learning and applying the skills taught in this book! The *Practical UX* process will be a methodology you can reach for again and again in the long career ahead of you. These skills will become ever more necessary as technology continues to outpace human ability. You have everything you need to build a foundation in accessible design and continue to become an expert in the field of accessibility and UX design.

CITATIONS

1. S. Byrne-Haber, "ADA Lawsuit Costs Are Way More Than Just the Settlement," *Medium*, Sep. 6, 2023. [Online]. Available: *https://sheribyrnehaber.medium.com/ada-lawsuit-costs-are-way-more-than-just-the-settlement-7f2aaccfe1e7*. [Accessed: Jan. 4, 2025].

2. K. Rivenburg, "Can you afford $25,000? Website accessibility lawsuits cost money," *Medium*, Feb. 9, 2023. [Online]. Available: *https://adabook.medium.com/can-you-afford-25-000-website-accessibility-lawsuits-cost-money-21987cd913f3*. [Accessed: Jan. 4, 2025].

3. CivicPlus, "DOJ's New Rule on Web Accessibility: What State and Local Governments Need to Know," *CivicPlus Blog*, Aug. 7, 2023. [Online]. Available: *https://www.civicplus.com/blog/wa/dojs-rule-web-accessibility-state-local-governments-need-to-know/*. [Accessed: Jan. 4, 2025].

4. European Commission, "Web Accessibility," *Shaping Europe's Digital Future*, [Online]. Available: *https://digital-strategy.ec.europa.eu/en/policies/web-accessibility*. [Accessed: Jan. 4, 2025].

5. U.S. Small Business Administration, "Justice Department Finalizes Rule Requiring State and Local Governments to Make Their Websites Accessible," *Advocacy*, Apr. 25, 2024. [Online]. Available: *https://advocacy.sba.gov/2024/04/25/justice-department-finalizes-rule-requiring-state-and-local-governments-to-make-their-websites-accessible/*. [Accessed: Jan. 4, 2025].

6. B. B. Murdoch, "The serial position effect of free recall," *Journal of Experimental Psychology*, vol. 64, no. 5, pp. 482–488, 1962.

7. AccessibilityWorks, "2023 ADA Website Lawsuits: Legal Statistics," *AccessibilityWorks Blog*, Aug. 23, 2023. [Online]. Available: *https://www.accessibility.works/blog/2023-ada-website-lawsuits-legal-statistics/*. [Accessed: Jan. 4, 2025].

8. ADA Site Compliance, "2023 ADA Web Accessibility Lawsuit Statistics: Full Report," *ADA Site Compliance*, 2023. [Online]. Available: *https://adasitecompliance.com/2023-ada-web-accessibility-lawsuit-statistics-full-report/*. [Accessed: Jan. 4, 2025].

9. G. A. Miller, "The magical number seven, plus or minus two: Some limits on our capacity for processing information," *Psychological Review*, vol. 63, no. 2, pp. 81–97, 1956.

10. N. I. Eisenberger and M. D. Lieberman, "Why rejection hurts: A common neural alarm system for physical and social pain," *Trends in Cognitive Sciences*, vol. 8, no. 7, pp. 294–300, 2004.

11. J. Jiang, "What I learned from 100 days of rejection," *TED*, Nov. 2015. [Online]. Available: *https://www.ted.com/talks/jia_jiang_what_i_learned_from_100_days_of_rejection*. [Accessed: Jan. 4, 2025].

12. WebAIM, "The WebAIM Million: An annual accessibility analysis of the top 1,000,000 home pages," *WebAIM*, Feb. 2023. [Online]. Available: *https://webaim.org/projects/million/*. [Accessed: Jan. 4, 2025].

13. G. Alexiou, "Website accessibility lawsuits rising exponentially in 2023, according to latest data," *Forbes*, Jun. 30, 2023. [Online]. Available: *https://www.forbes.com/sites/gusalexiou/2023/06/30/website-accessibility-lawsuits-rising-exponentially-in-2023-according-to-latest-data/*. [Accessed: Jan. 4, 2025].

14. UX Collective, "Case study factory: Avoid the pitfalls of templated UX portfolios," *UX Collective*, Sep. 1, 2023. [Online]. Available: *https://essays.uxdesign.cc/case-study-factory/*. [Accessed: Jan. 4, 2025].

*I*NDEX

www.ingramcontent.com/pod-product-compliance
Lightning Source LLC
LaVergne TN
LVHW062316060326
832902LV00013B/2248